TEXAS
DEPRESSION-ERA
DESPERADOES

TEXAS
DEPRESSION-ERA
DESPERADOES

Bartee Haile

Charleston London

THE
History
PRESS

Published by The History Press
Charleston, SC 29403
www.historypress.net

Front cover, top, left to right: Henry Methvin. *Courtesy of Texas/Dallas History and Archives Division, Dallas Public Library*; Marie Barrow. *Courtesy of Houston Public Library HMRC*; Harry McCormick with black eye. *Courtesy of Houston Public Library HMRC*; *bottom*: Bonnie and Clyde death car.
Back cover, top to bottom: Happy Bonnie and Clyde; Sam Maceo at New York narcotics trial. *Courtesy of Houston Public Library HMRC*; Female defendants at "harboring" trial.

First published 2014

Manufactured in the United States

ISBN 978.1.62619.227.0

Library of Congress CIP data applied for.

For Gerri, a wonderful wife and the love of my life

Contents

Introduction

O ver the years, I have lost count of the number of times someone has asked, "When are you going to write a book?" My stock answer was something along the lines of, "When I find a subject worth writing about that has not been written to death." After all, I usually added, there are more than enough biographies of Sam Houston and rehashes of the Alamo. Until then, I would be perfectly happy turning out my newspaper column, "This Week in Texas History."

Then one day in the winter of 2013, I received an e-mail from Christen Thompson asking if I might be interested in writing a book for The History Press. That got me to thinking, and to make a long story short, *Texas Depression-Era Desperadoes* is the end result.

Why a book about Texas outlaws of the 1930s? First and foremost, it was a fundamentally different time that produced a fundamentally different kind of lawbreaker. The Great Depression was an economic and social calamity the likes of which present-day Americans cannot comprehend. Millions had no roofs over their heads, no means of support and no idea where their next meal was coming from. There was no "safety net," and people kept falling until they hit rock bottom.

My maternal grandfather was one of those unfortunate individuals. He owned a small fleet of taxicabs in Big Spring, Texas, until he lost everything in the "Crash of '29." Daddy Jeffers (that's what I grew up calling him) walked the seventy-odd miles from Big Spring to Lubbock in search of work. For the rest of his life, he drove a cab around the streets of Lubbock from sundown to sunrise five, six and sometimes seven nights a week. And, yes, I am sure the irony was not lost on him.

Well, you could say, your grandfather found a way to survive the Depression without stealing and killing, and the criminals of that period could have too. Quite true, but that's not the point, is it? Each and every outlaw had his or her own personal reasons for turning to a life of crime, and that is what this book is all about.

If the characters in *Texas Depression-Era Desperadoes* break out of the one-dimensional stereotype in which they are so often trapped and spring to life as flesh-and-blood beings, I accomplished what I set out to do. And if you enjoy reading their stories, that's even better.

Chapter 1
West Dallas

WHERE THE WILD WEEDS GREW

If Clyde Barrow and the other Depression-era desperadoes who gave lawmen fits and took fellow Texans' minds off the hard times were to return on a day pass from the hereafter to the scene of their crimes, they would not recognize present-day Texas. But to understand the generation of young outlaws that ran wild in the Lone Star State during the 1930s, you must take a hard look at the Texas of their birth and upbringing.

Texas in 1910, the year Clyde Chestnut Barrow was born at a wide spot in the road south of Dallas, was a rural state of just under 4 million with four out of five living on small farms or in towns with populations under 2,500. Texas would, in fact, remain a majority rural state until the census of 1950.

Compare the Texas of 1910 with Texas exactly a century later. Today there are twenty-five million inhabitants, with three out of four residing in the "Big Triangle" formed by the Dallas–Fort Worth Metroplex at the northern apex; Houston, the fourth largest city in the United States, at the southeastern point; and San Antonio–Austin at the southwestern point.

Bonnie, Clyde and the rest of the colorful cast would be lost in this congested urban sprawl, but they would feel right at home in the sparsely settled countryside. Out in those wide-open spaces, there are still plenty of places to hide from twenty-first-century crime fighters in spite of all their newfangled technology.

In December 1891, Henry Barrow, a native of Florida who migrated to East Texas by way of Arkansas, made Cumie Walker, a local girl, his wife. Both were sixteen, marrying age at the time. Henry, who had seen the inside of a classroom for less than a full day in his whole life, could neither read nor write. Cumie, on the other hand, had attended school on a regular basis for a number of years and would insist upon their children learning the three Rs.

Soon after tying the knot, Henry quit his job at a Nacogdoches sawmill to chase the dream that would haunt him for the next thirty years. He rented several acres in the woods outside town, and the young couple started raising crops and having children—future free labor so essential to family farming. It never occurred to Henry to do anything else. He was, after all, following in the footsteps of his widowed father, who had put food on the table and clothes on the backs of his two sons by scratching out a living on someone else's land. What Henry had no way of knowing was that he had grown up seeing "tenant farming" at its best. But in the decades to come, he would experience the worst of a system that was a cruel sucker's bet, pure and simple.

In the economic aftermath of the Civil War, plantation owners across the Old South and in Texas, the westernmost member of the conquered Confederacy, were hard pressed to replace the emancipated slaves with the cheapest possible labor. They devised the fiendishly clever system of so-called tenant farming that tempted poor whites and poorer blacks with a pie-in-the-sky promise that never came true. As it evolved in Texas in the last third of the nineteenth century, tenant farming came in two flavors: share tenant and sharecropper. The share tenant supplied everything he needed (livestock, implements, feed, seed, whatever) to plant and harvest a crop, usually cotton. A third or a fourth of the crop went to the absentee landlord, and the farmer kept the rest for himself. The sharecropper, by comparison, brought nothing to the arrangement but the sweat of his brow. He was strictly "hired help" whose compensation was a portion or "share"—hence the name—of the crop, significantly smaller than the share tenant's. Both types of tenant farmers were at the mercy of the elements and the market. Drought, boll weevils, hailstorms and other natural disasters often left them with nothing to take to market. In those cases, they were compelled to borrow money at exorbitant interest rates, sometimes as high as 100 percent or more, to keep from starving and survive until the next planting.

Nevertheless, the percentage of Texas farms tilled by tenants steadily increased despite the mounting evidence that the deck was stacked against them. By the turn of the century, half of all farmers in the Lone Star State were tenants. The possibility, however slim, that they might someday put aside enough money to buy their own little piece of land gave thousands of Texans like Henry Barrow a reason to hang on no matter what.

In 1900, all the Barrows had to show for nearly a decade of struggle and sacrifice were two children: Elvin, better known as Jack, born in 1894, and a daughter named Artie, who followed five years later.

Instead of cutting their losses and finding a new line of work for the breadwinner, the Barrows packed their precious few possessions and moved to Milam County in the south-central part of the state. But things went from bad to worse, and the whole family, adults and small kids, occasionally had to hire out as day laborers on neighboring farms just to survive. On top of that, Henry and Cumie added two more growling stomachs: Ivan, whom everyone called Buck, and a second girl, Nell. When the Barrows finally faced the fact that there was no future for them on the rented acres in Milam County, they again had the opportunity to escape the tenant-farmer trap. But once again Henry decided that all they needed was a fresh start on a new piece of land.

Life did improve on the third farm six miles from Telico, a hamlet south of Dallas. That was where Clyde made his entrance in 1910. Every son had to have a nickname, and his was Bud. When the fourth boy joined the brood in 1913, the weary parents were down to initials. But L.C. was a heck of a lot better than his everyday moniker of "Flop," an insensitive description of his ears. Then, in 1918, at the age of forty-three, Cumie gave birth to her seventh and final baby, a third daughter they named Marie.

World War I was the closest Henry ever came to realizing his dream. With the fields of Europe full of trenches, machine guns and corpses instead of the usual bounty of a thriving agriculture, the demand for American cotton and other staples went through the roof. For the first time in their hardscrabble existence, the Barrows wound up with a little extra cash for luxuries like store-bought clothes for the younguns. With none of their draft-age sons risking his life in the bloodbath overseas, Henry and Cumie would look back on the war years as the good old days.

Peace in Europe did not bring prosperity to the cotton patch in Texas and the Deep South. Before the ink had dried on the Treaty of Versailles in the summer of 1919, the bottom dropped out of the cotton market, driving the price per pound down from a wartime high of forty cents to eight. The consequences for the small cotton farmer, especially of the tenant variety, were catastrophic. In Texas and elsewhere, seed cost more than the expected yield could bring. For farm folk at the mercy of market forces, the aftermath of the armistice amounted to a head start on the Great Depression a decade down the road.

If there ever was a time for Henry Barrow to call it quits, it was right then and there. But quitting was out of the question for a man with a lion's share of pride bordering on self-destructive and a stubborn streak a mile wide. Rather than join his neighbors in the mass exodus to the city, he chose to work part time in town, leaving Cumie and the children still at home to take up the slack in the fields.

That, however, was much easier said than done with the four oldest offspring long gone. Jack, Artie, Buck and Nell had left home, with the backbreaking drudgery and spirit-sapping poverty, for the bright lights of Dallas. And with the exception of Buck, who preferred stealing to working, they were doing just fine.

By 1922, even an illiterate like Henry could read the writing on the wall. He might have stayed on the farm and starved to death, but he did not have the right as husband and father to subject long-suffering Cumie and the kids to such a fate. The dream was dead, and it was time to go.

The five Barrows, two worn-out parents pushing fifty and three rambunctious youngsters between the ages of twelve and four, arrived in Dallas by horse-drawn wagon with pitifully few dollars and no place to stay. The three older children may have been better off by comparison, but that did not mean they had room for five long-term guests. There was a place for rural refugees with barely more than the clothes on their backs. In West Dallas, a squatters' slum on the "other side" of the Trinity River, Henry and Cumie joined countless other clans in the same dire circumstances. They camped out under an overpass, known in those days as a viaduct, where Cumie cooked over an open fire and everyone slept together under the wagon.

West Dallas was a community in name only. It was unincorporated marshland with no paved streets, no electricity, no running water, no sewer system, none of the standard services the respectable residents of Dallas took for granted. The city fathers in their comfortable downtown offices a short walk over the viaduct were under no legal obligation, much less the slightest political pressure, to change that shameful status quo, so they looked the other way. The worst slum in the state of Texas stayed frozen in time until the 1950s, when long-overdue annexation at last took the "West" out of West Dallas.

There was no prospect of gainful employment for a forty-seven-year-old illiterate sodbuster who had spent his entire life chopping cotton. But Henry Barrow was a survivor and grimly determined to play the part of provider until the final curtain. Making do with what he had, an old plow horse and a wagon, he picked through other people's trash for scrap metal, which he turned around and sold to the smoke-belching factories and foundries in Cement City next door to West Dallas.

Houston Street viaduct in 1922, the year the Barrows arrived in Dallas. *From the collections of Texas/Dallas History and Archives Division, Dallas Public Library.*

Neither the broiling heat of the Dallas summer nor the blue northers for which North Texas has always been so well known kept Henry from his daily rounds. He did not make much, pocket change to be truthful, but it was enough to improve the Barrows' diet and to buy the nails he used to build a shack out of scraps of discarded lumber. When he finally finished, the family of five had a roof over their heads for the first time since leaving the farm.

Tragedies rarely have a silver lining in real life, and given his track record, Henry Barrow had no reason to think he would be the exception to the rule. When a car struck and killed his horse in late 1929, he did not know where to turn until someone, maybe one of his grown children, suggested a lawyer. The threat of a suit was all it took to make the driver reach for his wallet, and suddenly the ex-sharecropper had more money than he had ever seen at one time in his life. He went right out and bought a Model T truck, his first and only motor vehicle, which quickly paid for itself in bigger and more frequent scrap-metal deliveries.

Two years later, again with the help of the older children, Henry acquired a couple vacant lots on West Dallas's main road. He moved the handmade shack from underneath the viaduct, the Barrows' address for the past nine years, to the site and turned it into a live-in gas station with two pumps. Gasoline sales proved to be disappointing, but the bootleg beer and moonshine he brewed on the side more than made up for it. Soon, the family had something they could really be proud of—a private outhouse out back.

At first Clyde shuttled back and forth between West Dallas and his uncle's place in Corsicana. To his mind, the new accommodations under the viaduct were a step down from the farm. So when his mother, out of fear that he would fall in with "the wrong crowd," suggested staying with his uncle, he jumped at the chance to return to the friends and familiar surroundings of his childhood.

By 1925, Clyde was back in the city to stay, and there was nothing Cumie could do about it. However, mustering her maternal powers of persuasion, she did succeed in convincing her fifteen-year-old to continue his education at a high school within walking distance of the campsite. Clyde went through the motions for a year or so, although he took a detour into downtown as many mornings as he made it to class, and in the spring of 1926, he gave up the pretense altogether. His mother had to have been disappointed by his decision to drop out, but she could not have been surprised. And there was no sense in arguing that a high school diploma would help him one bit in finding a better job, because they both knew that simply was not true.

That Clyde chose honest work over petty thievery revealed a lot about his core values and view of the world at sixteen. There can be no doubt that he had gone along on chicken-stealing escapades with his new West Dallas acquaintances and that he had no illusions about how older brother Buck seemed to have a pocketful of money without punching a clock. He may not have believed deep down that the best way to get ahead in life was to play by the rules, but he was willing to give it a try.

Clyde's employment record showed jobs were not hard to come by for a teenager who could read and write and had a quick mind to boot. He started at the bottom, earning a dollar a day at a cracker and candy factory before moving up to thirty cents an hour at the Procter & Gamble plant. He was training to be a glazier with a glass maker when he got into trouble with the law.

Clyde had fallen head over heels in love with a high school girl, and she felt the same. The couple planned to marry, apparently with the blessing of both pairs of parents. And why not? The young lovers were both sixteen! But in November 1926, they had a fight, and the girl, accompanied by her

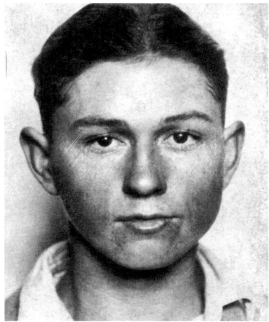

Top: Clyde Barrow and his mother, Cumie, the reason he stayed so close to Dallas. *From the collections of Texas/Dallas History and Archives Division, Dallas Public Library.*

Left: An early mug shot of Clyde, circa 1926.

mother, went to visit relatives in East Texas. Afraid he was on the verge of losing the love of his life, Clyde followed her in a rented car in order to kiss and make up.

His mistake was neglecting to inform the rental company he was leaving town with its property. When the deadline for the car's return came and went with no sign of the vehicle, the agency reported it stolen. Clyde evaded the sheriff's deputies that came to reclaim the car, but he was arrested for auto theft as soon as he showed his face back in Dallas. Legally, it was no big deal because the rental agency dropped the charges, leaving Clyde in the clear. But the problem for Clyde was that the police and sheriff's department now considered him a West Dallas "character" subject to the routine roundup of the "usual suspects."

Fifty-one years later, John Neal Phillips interviewed a close friend of Clyde's long-forgotten girlfriend for his book *Running with Bonnie and Clyde: The Ten Fast Years of Ralph Fults*. "After the ordeal with the rental car, he [Clyde] was fired from his job because the police kept picking him up," the woman recalled with impressive clarity after half a century.

"Whenever a car was stolen or a house burglarized, the police would drag him downtown. Of course, he was never charged with anything, but they'd beat him up and try to make him confess to things he'd never done.

"I still say that if the Dallas police had left that boy alone, we wouldn't be talking about him today."

Chapter 2

"From a Schoolboy to a Rattlesnake"

O ctober 29, 1929, was a bad day for the country and for the Barrow brothers. In New York City, the stock market, after teetering on the edge of disaster for the past three trading sessions, finally went over the cliff, sending share prices into a death spiral that doomed the U.S. and international economies to a decade of depression that only a world war could cure.

That very night, a stolen Ford slowed to a stop outside a mechanic's garage in Denton, north of Fort Worth. After a quick look around, Clyde and Buck Barrow and a casual partner in crime, whose name is not important, broke the lock and ransacked the premises looking for anything of value. A small safe caught their eye, but rather than take the time to bust it on the spot, they lugged the heavy metal box to the car and dropped it in the extra-roomy trunk.

On their way out of town, a patrol car pulled in behind the burglars and switched on the siren. Without a second thought, Clyde floorboarded the Ford, and the police gave chase. He was still in the Denton city limits when he lost control on a corner and slammed into a light pole. All three passengers were ejected from the getaway car by the force of the impact. They jumped to their feet and took off running with the cops hot on their heels. Shots rang out, and Buck collapsed in the street with bullet wounds in both legs. At the sound of gunfire, the third man stopped in his tracks, threw up his hands and waited for the breathless policemen to take him and Buck into custody. Clyde had better luck. He disappeared in the darkness, hid until the cops quit looking for him and hitched a ride to West Dallas.

Even though his brother faced an almost certain stretch in the penitentiary, Clyde was relieved to learn his wounds were not serious. While the news made him feel a little less guilty about abandoning Buck, he could not help but worry that the next knock at the door would be the Denton police come to fetch him.

The bungled burglary was not the only cause for concern. In the three years since the rental car fiasco, Clyde had been stealing more and working less. There was a long list of break-ins and car thefts that the law in half a dozen towns might connect to him at any moment.

Meanwhile, the wheels of justice spun mighty fast for Buck. A Denton grand jury indicted him for the garage burglary on December 6, and within two weeks, he was tried, convicted and slapped with a four-year prison term. The prospect of Buck doing hard time was depressing enough for Clyde, but the setting of a date for his Huntsville departure left the younger brother downright despondent. When the countdown reached nine days on January 5, 1930, a friend invited Clyde to a party, hoping to take his mind off Buck's plight at least for the evening.

Love at first sight is rarely a two-way street. Not so with Clyde Chestnut Barrow and Bonnie Elizabeth Parker. When they locked eyes that fateful night, the attraction was instantaneous, mutual and for the rest of their short lives. The strawberry blonde with the striking blue eyes was pretty in anybody's book. And for a young male sensitive about his height, Bonnie was the right size. At a fraction of an inch below five feet in her bare feet, she made Clyde, at five-foot-six, feel tall.

Because they had never met before that night, each presumed the other was new in town. But Bonnie had, in fact, been living in Cement City, the smokestack slum next door, for eight years longer than the Barrows had been in West Dallas. Like her new beau, she, too, was from the country. Born a year and a half after Clyde at Rowena due south of Abilene, at four years old, her life was turned upside down by the sudden death of her father in 1914. With three little children to support and no way to do it, Charles Parker's widow moved in with her parents in Cement City.

Cute, smart and talented—she could sing up a storm—Bonnie was the center of attention in every grade. The boys competed for her attention, and the girls were green with envy. She had everything going for her except a future full of fun, money and nice clothes. She was in her second year of high school when she fell head over heels for an older boy who promised her all that and more. So in September 1926, a week before her sixteenth birthday, Bonnie married Roy Thornton.

Bonnie Parker and her husband, Roy Thornton. She wore his ring until the day she died.

He was tall, good-looking and had plenty of cash to spend on his adoring bride, who did not think to question his source of income before tying the knot. But as Bonnie ultimately discovered, Thornton was a hard-core felon with lots of criminal irons in the fire that kept him away from home most of the time. The couple had been married a year when the husband pulled another of his vanishing acts without so much as a kiss goodbye. Bonnie was used to that by then, but as the days dragged into months without a word from Thornton, she reluctantly surmised he was gone for good.

After a yearlong absence, Roy Thornton put in one last appearance in January 1929. Bonnie, in the meantime, had made a life for herself waiting tables at a downtown café. For a pretty waitress who could flirt with the best of them, the tips were good. She told Thornton in no uncertain terms that they were through, an announcement he accepted with a shrug of his shoulders. That was the last time Mr. and Mrs. Thornton laid eyes on each other. Bonnie did not have to go to any great lengths to avoid coming into contact with her ex because that summer he went away for five years on an armed robbery rap. She never wrote Thornton in prison, but she never divorced him either. And she wore his wedding ring until the day she died.

Bonnie and Clyde became inseparable. Not only did they spend every waking hour together, Clyde usually stayed the night at her grandparents' place, sleeping on the couch. That was where he was when the long arm of the law reached out for him bright and early one morning in the second week of February 1930. The Dallas police had nothing on Clyde. They were merely doing a favor for their colleagues up north. So he twiddled his thumbs in the Dallas County jail until the Denton cops came for him.

Once again, Clyde got lucky in Denton. Citing a glaring lack of evidence, the grand jury refused to indict him on any charges stemming from the burglary that had landed Buck in the slammer. But that did not mean Clyde was free to go. Waco was next in line, and the district attorney was chomping at the bit to take a crack at him with seven open-and-shut cases, two counts of burglary and five of auto theft.

Realizing there was nothing to be gained by going to trial, Clyde threw in the towel and pleaded guilty on all counts. The judge gave him an automatic two years on each for a total of fourteen years, if served consecutively. But Clyde must have caught him in a good mood because he opted for concurrent sentences, which meant the first-time offender would be out in no more than two years. Any defendant in his right mind would have thanked his lucky stars for what amounted to a judicial slap on the wrist. But Clyde was not in his right mind. He was in love and could not bear the thought of being apart from the girl of his dreams for two weeks, much less two years.

A fellow prisoner approached lovesick Clyde with a plan to bust out of the McLennan County jail. All he had to do was persuade his girlfriend to retrieve a pistol hidden in his parents' house in Waco. Clyde did just that the next time Bonnie came to visit, talking her into committing her first major crime. Bonnie played her part to perfection and smuggled the loaded weapon into the jail without arousing the guards' suspicion. That night, March 11, 1930, the two prisoners surprised the guard delivering the evening meal and relieved him of his keys. In a matter of minutes, they were headed to Dallas.

The bold escape bought Clyde only seven days of freedom and no time at all with Bonnie. He was captured in Ohio and brought back to Waco to face the same judge, who reversed his previous sentence and "stacked" the seven terms. Clyde would spend the next fourteen years behind bars.

Clyde was going to a penal system that, in the words of the governor, was "not fit for a dog." With Texas prisons bursting at the seams with a third more inmates than it was built to accommodate, Governor Dan Moody on March 4, 1934, ordered all county sheriffs to hold onto their Huntsville-bound detainees until they heard otherwise. Six weeks later, Lee Simmons, who had taken over as general manager of prisons on March 25, declared he had found room for forty inmates. To his horror, Clyde learned he was one of the unfortunate forty.

Simmons talked a good game, good enough to convince a liberal like Moody that he was the man to weed out the brutality and sadism that had given the penal complex such a bad name, but he was no reformer. He was an

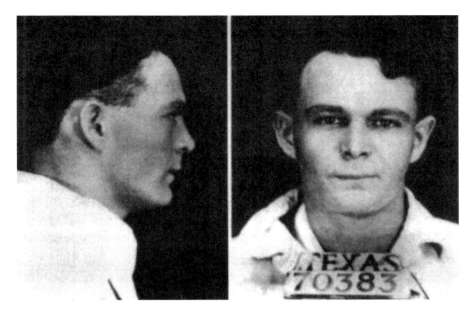

Ralph Fults in a Texas prison mug shot.

unapologetic advocate of corporal punishment "in the home, in the schoolroom, in the reformatory and in the penitentiary." That was the thinking behind his defense of the notorious "bat," a greased leather strap used in bloody floggings of inmates that tore their backs to shreds. He did not understand what all the fuss was about comparing the "bat" to the spurs that kept a horse in line. To enforce his get-tough policies, he quietly rehired the guards his predecessor had sacked for excessive violence and inhumane treatment of prisoners.

While waiting in the Waco lockup for the dreaded one-way ride to Huntsville, Clyde befriended an inmate with personal knowledge of the hellish ordeal ahead. Though a year younger than Barrow, Ralph Fults had been in and out of jail since he was fourteen. A native of Anna, a hamlet north of Dallas, he had a knack for escapes, his latest from solitary confinement at the infamous Eastham prison farm. But now he was going back.

In September, Clyde and his new pal arrived at "The Walls," the main prison in the middle of Huntsville, where they were processed and a few days later transferred to Eastham. Guards welcomed Fults home with a savage beating, standard punishment for returning escapees. Clyde watched with clenched fists as Fults was pistol-whipped and kicked with pointy-toed cowboy boots.

After a couple months, the prison staff decided to nip a potential escape risk in the bud by moving Clyde to the second Eastham work camp. Alone and without the hard-case Fults to watch his back, the scrawny youth was at the mercy of a vicious "BT" called "Big Ed." "BT" stood for "building tender," the name given to the hulking sociopaths who actually ran the prisons with the blessing of the guards and their superiors. Most were like "Big Ed," sadistic thugs whose street crimes had put them behind bars for the rest of their days.

"Big Ed," who carried 220 pounds of muscle on a six-foot, two-inch frame, preyed on Clyde for a year. Sometimes he beat him into unconsciousness, and other times he raped him within earshot of the other inmates, who dared not voice their objections or go to the screaming victim's aid.

Then in October 1931, another building tender with his own agenda came to Clyde with a proposal for dealing with "Big Ed" once and for all. He would not help him take his revenge, but he would take the blame, leaving Clyde in the clear. For the plot to work, Clyde had to make a tempting target of himself. He did this on the night of October 29, 1931, by getting out of bed and walking alone to the toilet in the inmate dormitory. His tormentor, who slept all day and prowled all night, was sure to follow.

"Big Ed" never saw the lead pipe in the skinny inmate's right hand. With a single blow, Clyde crushed his skull, killing him instantly. As soon as he was satisfied "Big Ed" was done for, the other BT emerged from the darkness, where he had watched the whole thing, and stabbed the dead man again and again with a shiv. Clyde went back to bed and listened to his accomplice give the guards a blow-by-blow description of a fictional knife fight that ended in the death of "Big Ed."

Prison officials went through the motions of investigating the incident and, on the recommendation of the guards at the scene, ruled it a simple case of self-defense. Clyde got his revenge, and the second building tender got "Big Ed" out of his life.

Two months later, in the last week of December 1931, Buck Barrow went back to The Walls to resume serving an interrupted sentence. In March 1930, just two months into his term, he had stolen a car belonging to a prison farm guard and driven away. His voluntary return had been prompted by pressure from his third and latest wife, a preacher's daughter named Blanche, who did not want a fugitive for a husband.

As soon as Clyde heard on the prison grapevine that Buck was in the Huntsville unit, he could think of nothing else but a brothers' reunion. Self-mutilation was the tried-and-true ticket off the Eastham farm and to a hospital bed inside The Walls.

On January 27, 1932, a cooperative convict took an axe to Clyde's left foot and hacked off the big toe and all or part of the next toe. He got his wish—a speedy trip to The Walls—but his timing could not have been worse, because six days later, the pardon his mother had worked so long and hard to obtain for her son came through. Clyde left prison on crutches, vowing never to return. He would die before he would go back to that kind of hell.

Half a century later, Ralph Fults told an interviewer that Clyde's time in Eastham changed him "from a schoolboy to a rattlesnake." Judging from the events of the next two and a half years, truer words were never spoken.

Chapter 3

Off and Running

BIRTH OF THE BARROW GANG

It took six weeks for word of Clyde's surprise pardon to reach Ralph Fults in McKinney. But as soon as he heard, Fults hopped the train to Dallas, stole a car for the occasion and drove straight to the Barrows' combination gas station/home in West Dallas.

Henry Barrow greeted the young stranger at the door. The family patriarch was cool and distant until Fults identified himself. "I'm Ralph Fults from McKinney. I done time with Clyde."

Henry nodded in recognition and said with a slight smile, "Clyde's been expecting you. Come on in. He'll be back from work soon."

Work? Fults nearly choked to keep from laughing. Clyde must have told his folks he was going straight and sold the story with a made-up job.

Fults wandered into the adjoining room, where three Barrows were huddled around a wood-burning stove on the cold winter day. Two—Clyde's youngest brother, L.C., and the baby of the family, Marie—were still in their teens, and the third was an attractive woman in her early twenties who obviously was not a Barrow by birth. She turned out to be Buck's new wife, Blanche.

Fults was casually shooting the breeze with the assembled Barrows when Clyde stormed into the house under a full head of steam. The "laws" had cost him another job, and it would be his last. Cumie entered the room, hoping to calm her hot-tempered son. Clyde gave his mother a hug and said in a hard, even tone, "Mama, I'm never going to work again, and I'll never stand arrest either. I'm not ever going back to that Eastham hellhole. I'll die first! I swear it! They're going to have to kill me!"

The die was cast. A life of crime and violence was not Clyde Barrow's destiny. It had not even been his first choice. But he had come to the fork in the road and found only one way open to him, and for better or worse, he was going to take it.

More than trust and the bond forged in prison brought Clyde Barrow and Ralph Fults back together. Out of their shared hatred of Eastham and a burning desire for revenge, an ambitious plan had evolved during long talks after lights-out in the prison farm dormitory. In fact, the plan to raid Eastham in the middle of the night may have been just plain crazy. Two groups of heavily armed ex-cons who knew the layout by heart would overpower the four sentries and storm the second-floor sleeping quarters where the rest of the guards were sawing logs. Once the guard force was disarmed and under their complete control, the raiders would release every single prisoner. The more they thought about it, the more convinced Clyde and Fults were that the plan could work. It was now a matter of recruiting the right men and raising the money for the necessary arsenal.

For their first job, Fults brought along a familiar face. He had met Raymond Hamilton in late January through the bars of the ancient jail in McKinney, but Clyde had known him for the better part of a decade. The eighteen-year-old owed his freedom to Fults, who smuggled the hacksaw blades to him that made his jailbreak possible.

Acting on information from an "inside" contact, the trio robbed the Simms Oil Refinery on the same road as the Barrow gas station on the night of March 25, 1932. Everything went as planned until Fults cracked open the safe. Instead of the company's fat weekly payroll, there was nothing inside. "The damned thing's empty!" Fults exclaimed in disgust.

The embarrassed robbers bound and gagged the four night-shift employees and retraced their steps to their waiting car. The only good thing about the Simms escapade was that no one recognized them, leaving the police with nothing to go on.

Barrow, Fults and Hamilton fared far better in a string of break-ins along Greenville Avenue. A couple corrupt Dallas cops not only scouted promising targets but also stood watch during the commission of the crimes. Even after splitting the proceeds with the crooks in blue, the safecrackers came out well ahead. But not nearly enough to finance the Eastham raid. That would take much bigger scores.

Five hundred miles north of Dallas, the threesome hit the jackpot in Lawrence, Kansas. The president of the First National Bank was a creature of habit with no sense of security. He opened the front door at the same time each morning and for the first ten minutes was all alone inside the bank. The bank president stuck to his routine the day of the robbery, but he was joined by two early-bird tellers. Clyde and Fults took the unexpected development in stride, and the robbery came off without a hitch.

They put off counting the money until safely inside a cheap hotel room in East St. Louis, Illinois. Clyde and Hamilton entrusted the tabulation of the take to Fults, but he had to tell them the amount twice before they believed their ears. The Texans were $30,000 richer. None of them had ever seen that much money in their penny-ante careers. Even divided three ways, it was a huge haul, and they had done it without harming a hair on anybody's head.

Hamilton's share was burning his pocket, and he could not wait to hit the highway for home. After exchanging a knowing glance, Clyde and Fults let him in on the Eastham plan. What they did not take into account was that the younger man had never done hard time, much less on the notorious prison farm, nor did he have any friends or kin on the inside. To risk his life on a suicide mission without any chance of a payoff made no sense to Hamilton, and he said so in the plainest possible English.

In no more time than it took to stuff ten grand in his pockets, Raymond Hamilton was out the door. But the day would come when he would find the Eastham plan just about the best idea he had ever heard.

In spite of Hamilton's defection, which Fults took better than Clyde, the pair returned to West Dallas in high spirits. Christmas came early for the Barrows and many of Clyde's friends, who were struggling just to keep their heads above water in the depths of the Great Depression. No one asked where the money came from. They were just grateful for the windfall.

After a few days of spreading their newfound wealth, the duo turned their attention back to the Eastham plot. New recruits were needed, and there was no better place than Denton to find them.

Clyde's key contact was a criminal veteran named Jack whom he and Buck had known since their chicken-stealing days in West Dallas. Jack recommended two younger crooks, whom Fults instantly recognized as members of his "graduating class" from the state reformatory at Gatesville. The third addition was Ted Rogers, a dead-ringer for Raymond Hamilton but his polar opposite in personality. While Hamilton was volatile, unpredictable and quick to fly off the handle, Rogers was calm, cool, collected and a killer.

As Clyde and Fults expected, the four ex-cons needed no convincing on the Eastham raid. In addition, impressed and inspired by the size of the Lawrence, Kansas take, the quartet was eager to duplicate that feat times two with the simultaneous robbery of a pair of banks on the Denton town square.

If Clyde needed any more reason to keep Ralph Fults at his side, he got it in dramatic fashion on the morning of April 11, 1932. As the other five men waited nervously in two cars, Fults took a precautionary stroll around the square. Even though he saw no cause for concern, he told his accomplices that he wanted to walk the same route one more time before giving the all-clear.

A minute or two into the second inspection tour, Fults spotted a showroom-new Chrysler sedan out of the corner of his eye. Crossing the street for a closer look, he realized the car was armor-plated, an expensive accessory only law officers and lawbreakers ever bought. That was enough to make his heart skip a beat, but the men in the front seat of the improvised tank took away his breath. Fults recognized two of the toughest Texas Rangers of the legendary corps: Tom Hickman and M.T. "Lone Wolf" Gonzaullas, the first Ranger with a Spanish surname. The half dozen desperadoes unanimously agreed to call the whole thing off. The odds may have been in their favor, but that was no advantage in a gunfight with Hickman and Gonzaullas.

Ralph Fults saved Clyde's life that morning in Denton, and he knew it. But eight days later, Clyde lost his right-hand man for good.

The happiest picture ever taken of Clyde and Bonnie.

Picture a Keystone Kops reenactment of the James-Younger Gang's Northfield, Minnesota raid. That's what it must have looked like the night of April 19, 1932, as Clyde, Bonnie and Fults tried to get out of a small East Texas town.

Passing through Kaufman in two stolen cars they had appropriated earlier that evening in Tyler, Clyde recalled a local hardware store stocked from floor to ceiling with guns and ammunition. Fults was working his magic on the back-door padlock when he heard gunshots from the front of the store. A night watchman who took his job quite seriously had traded shots with Clyde, who fired in the air to scare him off.

The watchman ran all right, but straight to the fire station, where he began ringing the alarm bell for all he was worth.

The center of Kaufman was filling up with sleepy-eyed inhabitants in their nightclothes when two cars sped past them on the highway out of town. But their fast-acting neighbors had blocked the exit with two road graders, forcing first Clyde and then Fults to reverse direction and go back the way they had come. A quarter of a mile later on the opposite side of Kaufman, the fleeing fugitives ran into another roadblock. They executed a second 180-degree turn and for the third time roared through town.

On this pass, Clyde spied a dirt road and disappeared in the darkness, closely followed by Fults in the second vehicle. But five miles from Kaufman, the escape route turned to mud, and both cars sank up to the axles in the sticky clay. The comic escape continued on mule-back with two animals from a frightened farmer, who did not have anything with four wheels and a motor. Riding into Kemp ten miles south of Kaufman half an hour before sunrise, they traded the mules for the village doctor's pride and joy, a brand-new automobile.

Understanding daylight would bring an army of trigger-happy vigilantes, Clyde took the highway southeast toward Athens. But the physician's car must have been running on fumes because it ran out of gas a mile from Kemp. Within the hour, the countryside was crawling with furious farmers and every able-bodied male from the offended communities of Kaufman and Kemp. Clyde, Bonnie and Fults spent the day hiding from the ever-larger posse that seemed to completely encircle them.

Late that afternoon, while it was still light, they chose to risk detection in order to break out of the trap. But an alert farmer sighted them and telephoned for help, bringing the entire posse down on them. The vigilantes soon were shooting at everything that moved. Fults took a .38-caliber bullet in the ankle but pressed on through the thick underbrush. A little while later, a second slug from a high-powered rifle severed an artery in his upper left arm. Clyde helped his companion slow the bleeding to a trickle with a tourniquet torn from Fults's shirt, but they both realized he was in no condition to keep on running.

Clyde whispered to Bonnie and Fults that he was going for help and would come back for them. Fults undoubtedly understood time was too short for such heroics, but he dared not say so in front of Bonnie, who was wide-eyed with fear. A minute or two after Clyde vanished from view, he ordered Bonnie to go on without him. In the event of capture, she was to play dumb and insist the big, bad bandits had kidnapped her.

And that was how Bonnie Parker and Ralph Fults ended up in jail together. The odd couple shared the same cell for that one night before being transferred to the county seat of Kaufman, which had separate accommodations for the sexes. That was Bonnie's home for two long months until the grand jury finally convened, concluded the case against her would not stand up in court and ordered her release.

It was a different story for Fults with no happy ending. He copped out on every charge stemming from the wild night and day in Kaufman County, and by May, he was penitentiary bound. Ralph Fults did not return to the free world until January 1935, after and Bonnie and Clyde were eight months dead.

During Bonnie's incarceration, Clyde kept busy with a string of nondescript holdups that netted not much more than meal and gas money. But an after-hours robbery that should have been a piece of cake went terribly wrong in Hillsboro on April 30, 1932.

Clyde stayed behind the wheel, while Ted Rogers and one of the Gatesville alums talked J.N. Bucher into opening his jewelry store. The white-haired merchant obliged the two customers, who had bought a guitar from him earlier in the day, but five minutes into the stickup, he made the mistake of reaching for a gun.

The loud report from a .45 was ringing in Clyde's ears when his two traveling companions jumped in the V-8 Ford. "That old man went for a damned gun!" Ted Rogers exclaimed with uncharacteristic emotion. "I had to plug him."

Bucher's widow watched the life drain out of her husband from the huge bullet hole in his chest. She positively identified, probably under coaching from the cops, Ted Rogers's lookalike, Raymond Hamilton, as the shooter. Raymond was not even in the state of Texas on the night of the Bucher homicide. With the Dallas police preparing to arrest him for the Simms Refinery job, he had skipped town two weeks earlier for his father's place in Michigan. Figuring three months was time enough for Dallas to cool off, he returned at the end of July to another man's murder charge.

Hamilton went looking for Clyde and an explanation. As soon as he heard Ted Rogers had pulled the trigger in Hillsboro, the misidentification made sense. But as long as he was wanted for murder, there was no reason to play hide-and-seek with the law.

Hamilton was ready for action, if Clyde had an opening. It was not a matter of letting bygones be bygones for Barrow. That was not his nature, and he had not forgiven Raymond for taking off after the Lawrence bank heist. But with Fults in the joint for who knew how long, he was short-handed and in no position to be choosy.

Adding a fresh face known only as "Ross," the reunited outlaws hit a meatpacking plant on the outskirts of Dallas the very next afternoon. The fact that the robbery occurred during regular business hours showed how much Clyde and Hamilton both needed the cash. Reports vary as to the amount of the take, but they may have gotten away with as much as $4,000.

Instead of sitting around Dallas to gauge how much heat the robbery had generated, the three drove to Oklahoma on August 5, 1932, picking up either a casual acquaintance or a hitchhiker on the way. Clyde, who never drank alcohol, turned a deaf ear to Ross's repeated requests to stop someplace where he could buy a bottle of moonshine, but passing through a speck on the map called Stringtown, he inexplicably relented and pulled into the parking lot in front of a dance hall.

Ross and the hitchhiker reappeared with hooch in hand but took a detour through the lot looking for a new set of wheels. Their suspicious behavior attracted the attention of Atoka County sheriff C.G. Maxwell and his subordinate, Eugene C. Moore, who thought the young strangers were nothing more threatening than a couple of teenage delinquents.

How and why the shooting started has been a subject of intense debate for seventy years. The undisputed facts are these: At some point, Clyde and Hamilton opened up on the two hick-town cops, killing Moore and crippling Maxwell. Fleeing the scene in a cloud of dust, they left Ross and his drinking buddy to get out as best they could. The unnamed suspect was promptly apprehended and just as promptly spilled his guts.

For the first time in their lives, Clyde Barrow and Raymond Hamilton were cop killers.

Stopping in Dallas only long enough to pick up Bonnie, Clyde drew a blank on their ultimate destination. Where could a pair of cop killers go to hide? In a flash, Bonnie had the answer: her aunt's farm outside Carlsbad, New Mexico, hundreds of miles from Dallas and the bloodstained Oklahoma parking lot.

Clyde, Bonnie and Hamilton drove straight through to the "Land of Enchantment," with timeouts restricted to gas stations and carry-out food. After a hard twenty-one hours, they reached their sanctuary, where Bonnie's trusting relative welcomed her niece and her two well-dressed friends with open arms.

A welcoming committee of a different kind came calling on Sunday morning, August 14. Chief Deputy Sheriff Joe Johns wanted to speak to the owner of the unfamiliar Ford in the driveway that happened to match a car reported stolen. Bonnie sweet-talked him at the door to buy time for Clyde and Hamilton to comb the house for some kind of weapon, as theirs were locked in the trunk of the car.

Deputy Johns wandered over to the Ford and was fiddling with the trunk when Clyde suddenly showed up with a sixteen-gauge shotgun. "Stick 'em up!" the Texas fugitive shouted.

Maybe it was Clyde's small stature, his young face or both that caused the New Mexico lawmen not to take him seriously. Whatever the reason, Johns went for the pistol on his hip and lost his hat to an expertly aimed blast from Clyde's shotgun. Knowing he was lucky to be alive, the deputy let go of his weapon and hoisted his hands.

Clyde marched his captive to the car as Bonnie and Hamilton rushed into the house to retrieve their belongings. After a polite thank-you to their stunned hostess for her hospitality, the three houseguests started the long trip back to Dallas with their New Mexico souvenir.

Clyde took a roundabout route through San Antonio, where the dazed but delighted deputy was deposited on a back road. Oh the story he would have to tell his grandkids of the ride he took with Bonnie and Clyde and how they treated him like family!

Clyde, Hamilton and even Bonnie, still regarded by the press and police as the female mascot of the Barrow Gang, were hotter than Fourth of July firecrackers for the rest of the year. But there were plenty of places to hide in West Dallas, as well as the kind of people who would have torn out their tongues before ratting on them.

On the night of January 6, 1933, two Tarrant County deputies, two Dallas County deputies, one "special Ranger" and an assistant DA from Fort Worth showed up uninvited at the West Dallas home of Raymond Hamilton's sister Lillian. They were trolling for a much smaller fish than the two most wanted men in Texas: an armed bandit who had taken $2,800 from a Cow Town bank.

Another Hamilton sister named Maggie informed the intruders that Lillian was out for the evening, and she was babysitting her children. Dallas deputy sheriff Fred Bradberry brushed her aside and seated himself at the front window. The prosecutor and a Fort Worth deputy staked out the back porch, while the two other officers kept Bradberry and the uneasy woman company in the parlor.

An hour went by with no sign of their prey or any useful information from Maggie. But around midnight, a car moving slightly faster than a snail rolled by the house once, then twice and on the third pass stopped out front. A man with his hat pulled down low over the upper half of his face emerged from the car and walked toward the door.

Bradberry growled at Maggie, "Open the door." She complied but screamed at the top of her lungs, "Don't shoot! Think of my babies!"

From under his long coat, Clyde Barrow whipped out a sawed-off, sixteen-gauge shotgun full of 00 buckshot. From a distance of ten feet, he unloaded on the silhouette in the window. The two lookouts on the back porch sprinted around the corner of the house. The unarmed DA let the deputy lead the way.

Clyde gave him fair warning: "Don't come any closer." The deputy took one more step, and it was his last. Clyde squeezed the trigger, sending nine pellets the size of small marbles into his heart.

Clyde was gone in a flash. He raced down the dark alley and rendezvoused with the waiting car on the next block.

Tarrant County deputy sheriff Malcolm Davis died en route to the hospital. Clyde Barrow was now a two-time cop killer.

Chapter 4

"Don't Get in That Car with Clyde"

Once Ralph Fults was back behind the high walls of the central unit in Huntsville, he made a point of looking up Buck Barrow. That was not hard to do since the older brother always seemed to be the center of attention.

Clyde and Buck were as different as night and day. Clyde was by nature a loner who smiled once in a blue moon and preferred to keep the world at a safe distance until he could determine whether someone merited his trust. Buck, in contrast, was an easygoing extrovert with a ready grin who never met a stranger and got along with everybody—no simple task in a penitentiary crawling with every kind of back-stabbing character under the hot Lone Star sun.

Toward the end of March 1933, Fults went to the exercise yard to stretch his legs. There was Buck with a bigger-than-usual smile on his face and a ring of inmates taking turns slapping him on the back and shaking his hand. It did not take long for Fults to fathom the reason for the celebration. Miriam "Ma" Ferguson, in her second and last term as governor of Texas, had granted Buck a full rather than a conditional pardon. When he walked out of the prison gates, he would be a free man with his record wiped clean of all prior arrests and convictions.

After the crowd thinned out, Fults took Buck aside to offer his personal congratulations and a prophetic piece of advice. "Don't get in that car with Clyde," he warned in an ominous tone that wrinkled Buck's forehead. "If you do, you're a goner."

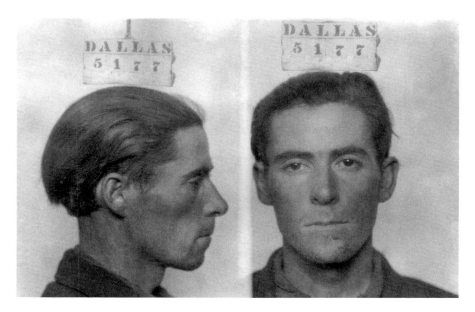

Buck Barrow ignored the warning not to "get in that car with Clyde." *From the collections of Texas/Dallas History and Archives Division, Dallas Public Library.*

Buck muttered, "I know. I know," and in the next breath launched into a rambling explanation of why Clyde was the first person he wanted to see after he got out. Buck's reasoning boiled down to this: since he was at best partly to blame for the trouble his baby brother was in, it was his responsibility to save him before it was too late. That meant talking Clyde into turning himself in and rolling the dice in court.

Buck's response, repeated word for word for the benefit of every person he came into contact with before and after his release, did nothing to reassure Fults or any member of the Barrow family. Blanche, the woman who had waited so patiently for him, shared their skepticism, but for the time being she was willing to take her husband at his word that he had put his lawbreaking past behind him.

In his younger days, Buck Barrow had blown through two marriages. His first produced twin boys, with one of the matching pair living less than a year and the marriage lasting not much longer. Buck's second attempt at wedded bliss was about as brief, with him also leaving wife number two something to remember him by—a baby girl.

Buck was between wives in November 1931, when he made the acquaintance of a pretty twenty-one-year-old preacher's daughter from

Oklahoma. Blanche Caldwell Calloway had run out on a bad marriage and was hiding out in West Dallas until her jilted spouse quit looking for her. Blanche's mother, who had been driven into the bed of a forty-year-old husband at the tender age of sixteen, apparently learned nothing from that train wreck of an arranged marriage. Mommy dearest forced her own daughter, just turned seventeen, into going down the same path with a man twice her age.

In no time flat, Buck and Blanche were madly in love and calling each other "Daddy" and "Baby." Sappy as those pet nicknames must have sounded, no one doubted their devotion. The moment Blanche's divorce became final, the love-struck couple hurried down to the courthouse. Buck had never listened to anybody in his life, but he listened to Blanche. The entire Barrow clan, including Clyde, was astonished when she persuaded him to go back to prison and finish the sentence interrupted by his escape two years before.

Buck's no-strings-attached pardon was the answer to Blanche's prayers. It was a chance for a fresh start, and she was not about to let him squander it. Then Buck told her that the first thing he had to do was find Clyde and convince him to give up his life of crime. The bombshell reduced Blanche to tears, and Buck spent their first night back together trying to get her to stop crying.

Clyde, Bonnie and W.D. Jones, the West Dallas teenager recruited over Christmas as a relief driver and second gun-hand, caught up with Buck and Blanche at the North Texas dairy farm owned by Blanche's mother and stepfather. Clyde turned on the charm for his sister-in-law, insisting the furthest thing from his mind was dragging his big brother into his hazardous life on the lam.

Blanche did not believe him for a second, but Buck did, and his commitment to straightening out his little brother was rock-solid and unwavering. When Clyde suggested a crime-free vacation, Buck told Blanche he was going whether she did or not.

For the getaway, Clyde chose Joplin in the southwest corner of Missouri, a hop, skip and a jump from the Oklahoma line. On April Fools' Day, the fivesome rented a two-story stone bungalow in a quiet neighborhood with living quarters above a garage with parking for Clyde's latest stolen transport and the four-door Marmon Buck had bought for the trip.

Bonnie looked forward to having another female around for a change, but that was before she got to know Blanche better. She learned to her dismay that Buck's stuck-up bride had packed more than her fair share of annoying

The Joplin bungalow today looks like it did before the 1933 shootout.

personality traits. Blanche looked down her nose at Bonnie, Clyde and W.D. and had as little as possible to do with them. When she was not complaining about the food, the accommodations and everything else that failed to measure up to her pretentious standards, she was bent over a magazine puzzle or petting her little dog.

Clyde and Buck spent their time playing cards, with W.D. occasionally sitting in when one of them spelled him on guard duty. Buck took advantage of breaks in the game to plead with Clyde to give it up before he got himself killed. Out of respect and affection for his sibling, who had his best interest at heart, the younger Barrow let the older have his say, but the conversation always ended the same. Clyde would remind Buck that cop killers did not go to prison, they went to the electric chair, and he would never let them strap him in "Old Sparky."

In advance of the trip, Clyde had told Buck not to worry about money, that he could count on him to pay for everything. But that was stretching the truth, and by the end of the first week in Joplin, cash was already in short supply. So Clyde and W.D. began going on late-night runs to replenish the treasury; the only person in the bungalow who did not know what they were up to was Blanche.

Buck disliked being left behind and, in spite of his recently turned-over "new leaf," soon joined Buck and W.D. on their nocturnal excursions. He rode along the night they broke into a National Guard armory and made off with a crate of Browning Automatic Rifles, a rapid-fire weapon capable of spitting out twenty high-velocity rounds in three seconds.

But it was not the rash of armed robberies in the area or even the unthinkable theft at a government arsenal that brought two Missouri state troopers and three Joplin policemen to the bungalow on the afternoon of April 13, 1933. In the mistaken belief that the target of the raid was nothing more threatening than a gang of bootleggers, the lawmen came armed only with their everyday handguns. It was reminiscent of the old joke about "taking a knife to a gunfight."

The three local cops parked one of their patrol cars at the curb and the other at an angle in the driveway, blocking the garage. The two troopers stopped down the street and were walking back to the assembly point when Buck raised one of the garage doors. "Laws!" he yelled, sounding the one-word alarm. Clyde and W.D. reached for their shotguns and turned toward the open door at the ready.

Wes Harryman could not see the shotguns trained on him or was in too much of a hurry to reach the dimly lit garage to notice. In the end, it made not a dime's worth of difference, as simultaneous blasts from Clyde and W.D. cut the constable down in mid-stride. With blood spurting from an artery in his neck, Harryman got off one shot before losing consciousness. He would die at the scene, not knowing he had hit W.D. Jones in the side.

Harry McGinnis, a Joplin detective, tried to complete his mortally wounded comrade's mission, but he, too, ran into the wrong end of Clyde's shotgun. The 00 buckshot nearly blew the plainclothes cop's right arm clean off at the shoulder, leaving it dangling by tendons and tissue. He hung on for the ambulance ride but died three hours later in the hospital.

As they passed on the stairs, W.D. handed his shotgun to Buck, who joined Clyde in keeping the three remaining cops pinned down. Meanwhile, the bleeding teenager helped the women prepare for immediate departure, telling them, "Leave everything!"

Doing as they were told, Bonnie and Blanche grabbed what they could carry and followed W.D. downstairs. He motioned for them to get in the back seat of the Ford sedan, and Bonnie did so, rolling into a tight ball on the floorboard. Blanche, however, suddenly noticed her fluffy white dog was nowhere in sight and wandered outside in search of him. Clearly in shock instead of hysterics, she walked by a state trooper who was too busy returning Clyde and Buck's fire to pay her any mind.

Buck raised the garage door in front of the Ford to find two obstacles blocking their escape route. He solved the first problem by dragging the constable's dead body off to the side. Clyde handled the second problem by ramming the police car in the driveway and propelling it into the street.

With a deafening roar from the Ford's powerful V-8, a blinding cloud of gravel and dirt kicked up by four spinning tires and a rolling stop to collect Blanche minus her dog, the Barrow Gang put Joplin in their rearview mirror. Intent on putting the state of Oklahoma between them and any possible pursuit, which never materialized, Clyde drove straight through to the Texas Panhandle, a distance of 450 miles. He pulled over only to refuel and to let Bonnie pluck a spent slug from his chest with her tweezers.

Back in the Joplin bungalow, the police marveled at the treasure-trove left behind by the Barrow Gang. There were suitcases full of women's dresses and men's suits, plus a purse containing irrefutable proof of the second couple's identity: their marriage license and Buck's pardon papers. W.D. was still the mystery man, but now "the law" at least had his picture.

Two exposed rolls of film turned out to be, in the modern-day parlance, a game-changer. There were enough snapshots of Clyde, Bonnie and W.D., taken with a cheap box camera on the side of an East Texas road a month or two earlier, to fill a family album. The police released the sensational photos to the *Joplin Globe*, which in turn made them available to newspapers across the country by means of electronic transmission over the newly established "wire services." Prior to their arrest, incarceration or death, the only glimpses most Americans had gotten of 1930s criminals were their mug shots. But there in black and white on the front page of the morning paper were three good-looking young outlaws clearly having the time of their lives.

The photographs captivated the public imagination, transforming an obscure band of small-time stickup artists no one had heard of outside of Texas and Oklahoma into a guilty pleasure. Dillinger, Pretty Boy Floyd, Machine Gun Kelly and the rest were pushed into the background by something new—two young lovers robbing and killing in a fast-lane ride to an early grave.

None of the Joplin photos had a greater impact than the one of Bonnie striking an exaggerated pose with a cigar in her mouth, a gun in her hand and her leg propped on a front bumper. To middle-aged, middle-class Americans,

John Dillinger objected to "a couple of kids stealing grocery money" pushing him off the front page.

who were weathering the Depression just fine, she was evil incarnate, "a cigar-smoking gun moll." But to the poor and unemployed falling through the canyon-wide cracks in the system, she was hundred-proof excitement and a source of vicarious revenge on the bankers and cops who had evicted them from their homes and farms and thrown their sons in jail.

Everything changed after Joplin. The "Barrow Gang" became "Bonnie and Clyde," and America could not get enough of them.

For the rest of April and all of May 1933, the Barrows and W.D. concentrated on staying out of sight by sticking to the country roads Clyde knew so well and steering clear of the bigger towns and cities. When they did come up for air, which was not often, it was to rob an out-of-the-way store, fill the tank or treat themselves to someone else's cooking in a roadside diner.

On the moonless night of June 10, 1933, Clyde was barreling down the highway seven miles north of Wellington on the eastern edge of the Texas

Panhandle. Bonnie sat alongside him, and W.D. was sound asleep in the back. Buck and Blanche had gone off on their own for a day or two but would rejoin them at a prearranged time and place.

Suddenly and without warning, Clyde ran out of road. The bridge over the Salt Fork River was gone, maybe washed away by a flash flood. If there was a warning sign, as some later claimed, Clyde did not see it in the darkness, and at seventy miles an hour, he could not have stopped in time. After a short but terrifying flight, the car landed on the concrete-hard riverbed and rolled over twice before coming to a stop on its roof. Clyde, who had been thrown clear but not knocked out, scrambled to his feet and ran to Bonnie's aid. W.D., also banged up but conscious, wormed his way out of the wreckage and began unloading their mobile arsenal.

A spark ignited a gasoline leak from the ruptured tank, setting the car on fire. W.D. dropped what he was doing and helped Clyde and two able-bodied farmers pull Bonnie clear before flames consumed the twisted mass of metal. Only their fast collective action saved her from burning alive.

The two first responders carried Bonnie the hundred yards to their farm with her screaming in pain every step of the way. Once inside, the seriousness of her injuries turned every stomach present. Acid from the car battery, not flames from the fire, had eaten away much of the flesh on her right leg from the hip down to the ankle. As W.D. later recalled, "I could see the bone in places."

Baking soda and salve applied ever so gently by the farmer's wife and daughter neutralized the acid and prevented even more extensive damage to Bonnie's leg. The vehicle driven by two curious country cops, drawn to the scene by the burning wreck, made it possible for the trio to get back on the road and keep their appointment with Buck and Blanche.

Clyde knew travel was out of the question until Bonnie's pain diminished and her condition improved. Five days after the accident, on June 15, he rented a double cabin in a "tourist camp" on the outskirts of Fort Smith, Arkansas, and put Bonnie to bed. He concocted a cover story about an oil-stove explosion to convince a doctor to make a house call. Hospitalization was the physician's preferred treatment, but he settled on a private nurse and prescriptions for the pain. Bonnie's suffering subsided, and she slowly started to heal.

To everybody's surprise, even Bonnie's if she had been clear-headed enough to notice, Blanche rose to the occasion. She took over the cooking and cleaning, which she thoroughly despised, and showed genuine compassion

"Pretty Boy" Floyd was not home when Bonnie and Clyde dropped by.

in the care she gave her bedridden traveling companion. And she did it all without her usual complaints.

The Fort Smith rest stop ended abruptly on June 23. Buck killed his first cop in a confrontation resulting from something as mundane as a traffic accident. Ready or not, it was time again to move.

During the next three weeks of meandering aimlessly across Oklahoma, Kansas and North Texas, Clyde showed up at the private residence of "Pretty Boy" Floyd in Salisaw, Oklahoma. The most wanted man in the Sooner State was not home, and his relatives who were could not have been pleased to find the notorious Texas outlaw on their doorstep. Clyde asked for Floyd's help in locating a "safe house," a request the woman in charge promised to pass along to "Pretty Boy." Nothing came of it, probably because Floyd had problems of his own.

Facing the fact that bed rest was the best medicine for Bonnie, the road-weary fugitives checked into a "motor court" on the main road six miles from Platte City, Missouri, on July 18, 1933. Blanche went into town for medical supplies with a shopping list that included syringes and a particular painkiller that had proven effective for Bonnie. The druggist who rang up the purchase telephoned the sheriff's office as soon as she walked out the door. In accordance with a multi-state alert, Holt Coffey wanted to hear about any strangers seeking potent pain medication, and Blanche Barrow fit that profile.

Unlike his counterparts in Joplin, Sheriff Coffey knew what he was going up against and resolved not to repeat their costly mistake. He issued an urgent call to arms to agencies in the area, as well as to the Missouri state police, and waited for the response.

At six o'clock the following evening, the working parts of a posse began coming together in the parking lot of the tavern across the highway from the motor court. At closing time five hours later, Coffey counted sheriff's deputies from three counties and a small contingent of highway patrolmen for a total complement of thirteen. They were to a man loaded for bear with submachine guns, hunting rifles, heavy iron shields, bullet-proof vests and an armor-plated car.

The plan was to wait for the popular tavern to clear out before taking action, but the customers refused to relinquish their ringside seats. At half past eleven o'clock, with civilian faces pressed against every window, the posse marched in formation across the highway behind the armored car. The driver stopped in front of the two-car garage as the dozen armed officers formed a semicircle in front of the two cabins. Blanche, the only one of the five still up, answered Sheriff Coffey's knock on the door with the obvious question, "Who is it?"

"I need to talk to the boys," was the understated reply.

"Just a minute," Blanche said, speaking in code. "Let us get dressed."

It may have been a lifetime of deeply ingrained courtesy, but the sheriff did as Blanche asked, motioned for the possemen to stay where they were and waited for the gang to "get dressed."

Clyde was out of bed in a heartbeat, grabbing the customized BAR he called his "scattergun" and barking orders to a groggy W.D. "That's the law! Get the car started!"

Clyde fired first, a brief burst through the wooden garage door that sent Sheriff Coffey diving for cover, and followed with longer bursts from each of the cabin's three windows that left the entire posse facedown in the dirt. Clyde then stepped out of the door and emptied the rest of his sixty-shot banana clip into the armored car. The steel-jacketed barrage from the BAR passed through the metal plates like so much Swiss cheese and skewered the driver's legs. The sudden and extremely painful realization that the vehicle afforded no protection whatsoever caused him to panic. He threw the armored car into reverse and, oblivious to the posse behind him, backed away from the garage doors and out of the line of fire.

With the armored car no longer in their way, all the outlaws had to do was pile into their cars and drive away just like they had in Joplin. With a superhuman effort, Bonnie limped to the garage and collapsed in the backseat just as W.D. turned the ignition on Clyde's car. Buck and Blanche were right behind Bonnie until the posse opened up with everything they had.

A bullet from a .45 hit Buck in the head, entering through the left temple and exiting the forehead after ricocheting around the interior of his skull. He dropped to his knees, stunned and disoriented but conscious and still breathing. Clyde grabbed one arm, and Blanche, who astonished everybody, including herself, by keeping her wits about her, grabbed the other and lifted Buck into the car.

Then came the life-or-death moment when Clyde backed the Ford out of the garage and into a firing squad. The posse peppered the car, shattering every window and filling the interior with flying shards. Jagged pieces of glass hit Blanche in the face, driving a large sliver deep into her left eye.

The Missouri lawmen were seconds away from closing the book on the Barrow Gang when they stopped shooting and let Clyde drive away. Did Sheriff Colley or someone else shout, "Cease fire," or did each would-be executioner make a personal decision to let the outlaws go?

After Platte City, Buck Barrow was living on borrowed time, and the loan came due five days later at an abandoned amusement park outside Dexter, Iowa. This time the posse, consisting primarily of overzealous civilians, was bigger and out for blood.

Compared to Joplin and Platte City, the so-called Battle of Dexfield Park was a battle in name only. In the early hours of July 24, 1933, the armed mob led by a dentist with a tommy gun tried to surround the Barrow Gang's campsite but never quite closed the circle. After a brief one-sided exchange, during which the outlaws sustained every bullet wound save one, Clyde, Bonnie and W.D. stumbled and fell toward a nearby river, leaving Blanche, who refused to budge from Buck's side, with her dying husband.

The trio made it across the waterway to a farm and a poor excuse for an automobile that was almost in worse shape than the three Texans. But Clyde and W.D. got it running and, while the mob was preoccupied with their two prizes, drove away as they had so many times before.

Blanche Barrow tried to go to dying Buck's side at Dexfield, but police held her back.

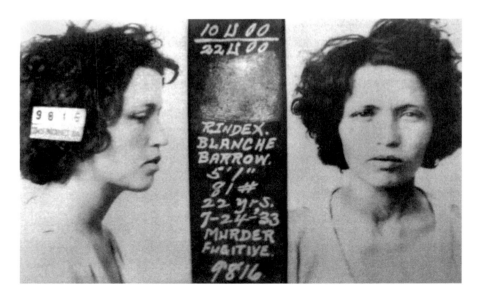

This Missouri prison photo shows Blanche's gaunt face after a drastic weight loss.

Buck underwent emergency surgery for a bullet that had pierced his back and lodged in his chest. The attending physicians removed the slug, but that did not improve their prognosis. Buck was bound to die from either the God-awful head wound or pneumonia.

With the help of Smoot Schmid, the recently elected sheriff of Dallas County, Cumie Barrow and her son L.C. were at Buck's bedside when he passed away on July 29. They took his body back to West Dallas, where he was buried two days later. They bought a plot next to Buck for Clyde and, with his permission, postponed the purchase of a permanent marker for the Barrow brothers to share until Clyde's time came.

Blanche Barrow never saw Buck again after she was whisked off to jail. She was not with her husband when he died, and authorities did not allow her to attend his funeral. Blanche pleaded guilty to the attempted murder of the Platte City sheriff, even though everyone knew Holt Coffey's superficial neck wound was caused by "friendly fire." She just wanted to get it over with and start doing her time: ten years in the Missouri state prison.

Chapter 5

The Teenage Tagalong

Nineteen-year-old L.C. Barrow spent Christmas Eve 1932 doing what he did most nights: driving his father's rattletrap around the back streets of West Dallas and drinking whatever bathtub spirit his corner bootlegger was selling. That holiday evening it was a caramel-colored liquid with a mule's kick that the youngest of the Barrow boys was told was whiskey.

L.C. did not mind what it was called as long as it warded off the cold and got him a little high. His passenger, who also went by his initials, was of the same mind. William Daniel Jones, who much preferred W.D., was only sixteen, but like his friend, he, too, had been drinking for years. It was just part of life in the West Dallas slum.

Recognizing his father's car, Clyde Barrow tailed L.C. for a block or two before honking at him to pull over. Clyde and Bonnie were back in town bearing Christmas gifts, and he told his youngest brother to fetch their mother and baby sister. Meanwhile, W.D. could wait with them.

Not knowing what, if anything, to say, Jones kept his mouth shut after he squeezed into the back seat next to the stack of firearms and boxes of ammunition. The sight of so many weapons aroused his natural curiosity, but he resisted the impulse to touch for fear of causing an accidental discharge.

L.C. returned with Cumie and Marie Barrow, who showered Clyde with kisses before opening their presents. Many tears and an hour later, he said it was time for Bonnie and him to leave, and his mother, sister and brother reluctantly headed for home.

When W.D. started to climb out of the back seat, Clyde asked him to stick around so they could talk. "We've been driving a long ways," explained the outlaw with dark circles under his eyes. "We need someone to keep watch while we get some rest." Stunned speechless by the invitation, the youngster accepted with an emphatic nod of his head.

From the adolescent's point of view, only a fool would have turned down the famous desperado. Clyde offered excitement, easy money and a way out of the grim poverty of West Dallas to a kid who had never worn anything other than hand-me-downs and considered himself fortunate to eat three meals in the same day. The risks paled in comparison to the rewards, or so it seemed on that chilly Christmas Eve.

The recruitment of W.D. Jones was not, in fact, an impulsive act on Clyde's part. He had known the boy since 1921, when their respective families—the Barrows from Telico south of Dallas and the Joneses from the East Texas county of Henderson—had camped out under the Houston Street viaduct. The most-wanted man in Texas needed somebody he could trust and felt in his bones that the hero-worshipping teen would stand by him come hell or high water.

Clyde put that opinion to the test less than twenty-four hours later. Although Temple, like all small towns on Christmas Day, was closed down for the holiday, he succeeded in locating a pharmacy open for business. Parking a block away, he handed W.D. a heavy revolver and snapped, "Follow me while I get us some spending money."

The tension mounted as the bandits waited for the proprietor to show his face. The experienced robber was as cool as a cucumber, but the novice lost his nerve and bolted out the door.

Clyde caught up with W.D. and gave him a stinging tongue-lashing that started with the three words "You yellow punk!" "I want to go home," the teenager whined with watery eyes. "Well, climb in that car," the veteran criminal sneered, pointing at a Model A, "and drive yourself back to Dallas."

The keys were in the ignition, but W.D. was so rattled that he could not get the cold engine to turn over. After signaling Bonnie to follow in the coupe, Clyde shoved him roughly aside and smoothly started the car.

Just as he accelerated away from the curb, Doyle Johnson leaped on the running board. The twenty-six-year-old salesman was not about to allow two punks half his size to steal the car he had scrimped and saved to buy.

Clyde yelled, "Get away, man, or I'll kill you!" Johnson ignored the threat that would have made most men's blood run cold and lunged at the thief through the open driver's side window.

"Stop or I'll kill you!" screamed Clyde, issuing his second and final warning as the salesman's fingers tightened around his neck.

When the outraged owner again paid no heed, Clyde raised his pistol and shot him in the throat. The wound proved fatal for Doyle Johnson, whose death the next day made his young wife a widow and left her with an infant to raise all by herself.

Clyde had no use for the Model A, which he ditched a half mile down the road in favor of the faster coupe he already was driving. W.D. curled up in the back seat and did not let out a peep for two hundred miles. He had witnessed his first killing, and it would not be the last.

Over the next two weeks, W.D. adjusted to his new life and everything that came with it. By the time the road warriors doubled back to West Dallas on January 6, 1933, he was happy and relaxed and addressing Bonnie and Clyde as "Sis" and "Bud," what he had called Clyde in those hard times under the viaduct before he ever heard his real name.

W.D. was in the car with Bonnie when Clyde walked up to the house of Raymond Hamilton's sister. The sound of gunfire and breaking glass jolted Bonnie into action, and she shifted into gear just as W.D. shot wildly at the house.

"Stop it!" she screamed. "You may hit Clyde." "Oh," was all W.D. could think to say, but he learned a valuable lesson that night, part of the on-the-job training for an apprentice outlaw.

At sunrise the next day, Clyde stopped for gas at an isolated station in northeastern Oklahoma, where he filled the tank and cleaned out the cash register. Tucking the eight dollars in his pants pocket, he promised to repay the "loan" provided the owner did not call the cops. Within the week, Clyde had rewarded the close-mouthed man for his cooperation with five crisp twenties. Similar episodes along with generous handouts to destitute farm families and the urban unemployed made for good press that fostered the public perception of the Barrow Gang as a merry band of modern-day Robin Hoods.

It was during the Joplin vacation and subsequent shootout that W.D. showed he could pull his weight. Clyde trusted him to keep watch without falling asleep and did not go anywhere without him, especially on the nightly robbery runs.

But it was W.D.'s courage and cool head under fire that impressed "Bud" the most. The sixteen-year-old did not let the bad bullet wound sustained in the opening moments of the gunfight with the Joplin cops knock him out of action. Many grown men would have been crying for

W.D. Jones (on right) posing with his hero, Clyde. In a suit and tie, Jones looked older than sixteen.

their mothers. Then there was the way he blocked out the pain and calmly led Bonnie and Blanche down the stairs to the getaway car, thereby expediting the escape. Yes, the kid really had what it took.

Except for an occasional groan, W.D. suffered in silence as Clyde drove the width of Oklahoma from the carnage in Joplin. He was certain there were two slugs inside him, but Clyde proved him wrong with an ingenious procedure. He wrapped a thin tree branch in gauze, doused it in rubbing alcohol and pushed the probe through the bullet hole and out the boy's back. The through-and-through wound healed nicely, thanks to "Doc Barrow."

W.D. more than repaid Clyde for the emergency medical care with his swift action the night of the Wellington wreck. If it had not been for W.D. and the two Good Samaritans from the nearby farm, Bonnie might well have burned to death.

He also kept his head in the highway confrontation with the two Arkansas lawmen that culminated in Buck's killing of H.D. Humphrey. Bullets and bloodshed were now so commonplace for the combat-hardened kid that losing the tips of two fingers to a lucky shot by the surviving cop did not even faze him.

W.D. took understandable pride in his indispensable part in Bonnie and Clyde's escape from the Dexfield shooting gallery. If not for his help, Clyde with his wounds and Bonnie with her crippled leg most likely would have drowned in the river or been captured along with Buck and Blanche.

Although W.D. stuck around six more weeks to care for his companions and handle all the chores, he had reached the limit of his physical and psychological endurance. He loved Clyde and Bonnie like brother and sister but not enough to die with them. They understood and did not resent or second-guess his decision to leave when the time finally came. In their last conversation, Clyde went over the "cover story" they had devised in the event of W.D.'s arrest. The most important thing for him to remember was that he never had been a voluntary member of the Barrow Gang but their prisoner compelled at gunpoint to commit the crimes the law tried to pin on him.

The parting took place in early September 1933, but historians and Bonnie and Clyde buffs disagree on where and how. Some contend it happened in Mississippi, where Clyde sent W.D. for gas and he never came back. That story does not hold water on several counts, first and foremost Clyde's reaction to his protégé's arrest and public statement. The more believable version is that Clyde and Bonnie simply dropped him off in West Dallas, where it all had started eight action-packed months earlier.

Whether it was Mississippi or Dallas, W.D. took a bus to Houston, where his mother had moved. Farm labor was one of many occupations in those days that did not require proof of identity or a background check, so the baby-faced fugitive had no trouble finding work picking cotton. In early November 1933, about the time he was beginning to believe the law had forgotten about him, a Dallas County deputy sheriff collared him in the field.

Sheriff Smoot Schmid wanted to squeeze every bit of information out of his prized prisoner before breaking the news that he had a member of the Barrow Gang in custody. At first, Schmid was pleased that W.D. was willing to talk, but he realized after a couple of long interrogation sessions that the captive was reciting a prepared story that revealed next to nothing of importance.

W.D.'s biggest worry was that he might be extradited to Arkansas to stand trial as an accessory to the murder of H.D. Humphrey. Even though Buck had pulled the trigger, his presence made him eligible for the death penalty under Arkansas law. Aware of W.D.'s concern, Schmid offered him a deal. If he would open up and plead guilty to the double murder of the cops the previous January, the sheriff swore he would serve his sentence in Texas and never set foot in an Arkansas courtroom. W.D. signed the plea agreement on the dotted line but never really spilled

W.D. Jones in the Dallas jail following his capture. *From the collections of Texas/Dallas History and Archives Division, Dallas Public Library.*

his guts. All the sheriff got in return was an embellished version of the teenager's original tale.

While Schmid went around and around with the tap-dancing prisoner, the chance to capture W.D.'s running mates fell into his lap. The ambitious sheriff once said in the presence of Deputies Ted Hinton and Bob Alcorn that if he ever had Bonnie and Clyde in his clutches, he would "walk them down Main Street in Dallas to show the world what I've done." The feat would be his ticket to the top rung of the political ladder, which in Texas meant the governor's office.

After receiving an anonymous tip on the exact location of a Barrow-Parker family gathering on November 22, 1933, Schmid and four deputies packing a BAR, two submachine guns and a rapid-fire rifle lay in wait. Despite vigorous protests from Hinton and Alcorn to the contrary, the sheriff had gotten it into his head that Clyde Barrow would give up without a fight.

Clyde's trademark Ford V-8, this time a sedan, came rolling down the road right on schedule. But as he approached the parked car with both mothers, two sisters and a family friend, he sensed something was not quite right and stepped on the gas.

Gone in an instant was Schmid's golden opportunity to take Bonnie and Clyde alive. He made the snap decision to settle for the next best thing and shouted for his men to open fire. The four weapons roared in unison, pockmarking the V-8 and the relatives' vehicle too, which was in the line of fire across the road. Incredibly, no one was hit in the second car, but a bullet from the BAR passed through the legs of both Bonnie and Clyde. However, the wounds did not impede their escape. The sheriff stood in the road, dumbfounded and cursing his luck. He had missed his chance, and there would not be another.

Newspapers in the 1930s did not pull any punches in their coverage of law enforcement. The Dallas dailies took unrestrained delight in raking Schmid over the coals with front-page articles like the one that opened with this zinger: "Evading, as has become a habit of his recently, a trap laid for him by Sheriff Smoot Schmid, Clyde Barrow…fled in a machine gun bullet-riddled car." All the subject of the ridicule could say in his own defense was, "At least we didn't get any of my men killed like they did up in Missouri."

To change the subject and divert attention from his humiliating failure, Sheriff Schmid trotted out his secret prize, W.D. Jones. For days, the papers ran stories of the terrified teen's ordeal as a captive of the Barrow Gang, how he was kept under guard and chained to bedposts at night by the heartless bandits.

Clyde took W.D.'s performance in stride and went so far as to note approvingly that he "played it smart." His sole concern was how high a price his boyhood buddy would wind up paying, and Clyde would have been happy to hear W.D. got off with fifteen years. Even if he had to do the full stretch, which was highly unlikely, the tagalong teenager would be as free as a bird before his thirty-first birthday.

Chapter 6

The Raid on Eastham

In the aftermath of the botched ambush on November 22, 1933, Sheriff Smoot Schmid figured Clyde Barrow and Bonnie Parker had lit out for parts unknown and would not risk showing their faces anytime soon in West Dallas. This opinion, shared by every lawman in Dallas except the two deputies who knew them best, did not take into account the freedom with which the couple was able to move in and out of their home base.

An exact record of her son's visits that Cumie Barrow kept on a wall in the family gas station/home provided proof of the ease and frequency of his movements. Clyde returned on November 29 to see for himself that his mother had not been wounded in the reckless crossfire seven days earlier. He came back five more times in December, never going more than nine days between visits, and on six separate occasions in January 1934.

Clyde's uncanny ability to come and go as he pleased in his boyhood slum was common knowledge in the joint. Five months into a stack of sentences totaling 263 years, Raymond Hamilton was learning from personal experience why Clyde hated the Eastham prison farm with such a passion. The plan he had dismissed as a good way to get killed now looked like his express ticket out of the hellhole.

Raymond sent a five-time loser named James Mullen, who finished his latest sentence on January 10, 1934, out the front gate with a message for his brother Floyd. It took Mullen, a falling-down drunk and drug addict, two days of wandering door to door in West Dallas to locate the older Hamilton but only twenty-four hours for Floyd to set up a clandestine conference with Clyde.

Bonnie could tell from the frown on Clyde's face what he thought of Raymond's self-centered revision of the bold plan for the Eastham breakout he had patiently pieced together with Ralph Fults. She liked the idea for no other reason than it would replenish their ranks. Without Buck, Blanche and W.D., the Barrow Gang was down to the two of them, and it would take an infusion of fresh blood to resume robbing banks.

Raymond's plan called for stashing two Colt .45-caliber automatics with ample ammunition on the edge of the Eastham farm. A trusty would bring the weapons to Joe Palmer, a thirty-one-year-old asthmatic bank robber, who would hold onto them until the morning of the escape. Raymond, Palmer and Ralph Fults would surprise the guards and race through the thick woods on foot to the road, where Clyde and Bonnie would be waiting with the motor running.

Clyde's initial reaction was to tell Floyd Hamilton to forget about it. Why should he take a chance like that for three cons that included only one, Ralph Fults, whom he knew and cared about? Floyd responded by taking him on a guilt trip. Clyde owed it to Raymond for the simple reason that a giant chunk of his two-and-a-half-century rap was Ted Rogers's murder of the Hillsboro storekeeper.

Clyde stepped out of the car and paced back and forth in the darkness. When he slipped behind the wheel, he had reached a decision. Yes, he would do it, but on one condition: Floyd and Mullen had to be the ones to hand-deliver the guns. After all, Clyde emphasized, Raymond should be willing to share in the risk for the sake of his own flesh and blood.

So in the wee hours of Sunday, January 14, Floyd Hamilton and the basket case Mullen left the guns and ammo wrapped in an inner tube under the designated bridge. Later that day during regular visiting hours, Floyd informed his brother of the deposit and went over the escape plan. Raymond grunted in approval and said for him to tell Clyde to be ready and waiting at first light on Tuesday morning the sixteenth.

Later that afternoon, Fults was abruptly transferred out of Eastham. Cursing his lousy luck, he implored Raymond to take Hilton Bybee, a convicted killer, in his place. Hamilton agreed to honor his request, keenly aware that Clyde would be infuriated by the last-minute switch. However, Barrow would not know Fults had been scratched until he was a no-show at the departure point and it was too late to back out.

The trusty brought the weapons cache to Joe Palmer on Sunday night. The next morning, he faked an asthma attack to get out of going to work. The guard, who gave him permission to stay in bed, did not think twice about it or he would have checked the chronically ill inmate's bunk.

Raymond Hamilton and Joe Palmer were each packing a loaded .45 as they shuffled to the field on the morning of January 16, 1934. Raymond made sure Olin Bozeman, the guard in charge of his work detail, saw him break ranks and join Palmer's group. Bozeman waited until the convicts arrived at their work area before summoning "high rider" Major (his first name, not his rank) Crowson.

The two were discussing Hamilton's infraction when Palmer sauntered over to them as if to ask a question. Palmer stopped within six feet of the guards and shot Crowson once in the gut. The "high rider" pitched forward from his horse, pulling the trigger of his shotgun as he fell to the ground, but the blast blew harmlessly through the treetops. Then either Palmer or Hamilton took out Bozeman with a bullet to the hip, and the race was on.

Raymond, Palmer and Hilton Bybee ran as fast as their legs could carry them through the thick early morning fog. Not waiting around for an invitation, two fast-thinking convicts joined them: Henry Methvin, a Louisiana bruiser doing a decade for attempted murder, and J.B. French, a crook from Oklahoma who had spent most of his adult life behind bars.

Bonnie leaned on the horn to direct the escapees through the fog, while Clyde provided cover fire with his ever-ready BAR. Guards and convicts buried their faces in the soft soil at the terrifying sound of the automatic rifle. As soon as it dawned on them the invisible sniper was shooting over their heads, two of the three guards and many of the inmates dashed for home. The remaining guard was made of sterner stuff and single-handedly stopped the mass escape Clyde Barrow and Ralph Fults had once envisioned.

Four of the five runaways reached the car. French thought better of crashing somebody else's party or felt flying solo improved his chances. Either way, he had it wrong, because the guards who combed every square foot of the woods uncovered his hiding place around midnight.

Clyde's V-8 was a two-door coupe with barely enough room for five small adults. Mullen took one look at the burly Methvin, a head taller than the rest of the prospective passengers, and declared only Raymond and Palmer were making the trip.

Clyde ordered Mullen to shut up, that it was his car and the decision was his. Under no circumstances would he leave anybody, friend or stranger, behind. Two men climbed in the trunk, and the other three squeezed into the Ford with Clyde and Bonnie. Clyde deftly navigated the twists and turns of the one-lane road, executing a getaway that was as clean as a whistle.

Six or seven hours later, between Fort Worth and the Red River, Clyde phoned the Barrow residence, where L.C. and Floyd Hamilton were

Clyde holds the BAR "scattergun" he used to provide cover for the Eastham escape.

waiting for his call. He gave them a time and place to meet with fresh clothes for the jailbirds, who were still wearing their prison-issue garb. Raymond, Palmer, Bybee and Methvin changed in the car, and L.C. and Floyd drove back to West Dallas with Mullen, who was instructed to get lost permanently.

The first item on the "new" Barrow Gang's agenda was the $1,000 owed James Mullen for services rendered in the preparations for the breakout. Raymond and Bybee walked out of a small-town bank in the northwest corner of Iowa with Mullen's grand and an extra $2,800.

Sick as a dog with fluid-filled lungs and bleeding ulcers, Joe Palmer slept through the heist. When the time came to divvy up the profit, Clyde awarded Palmer a full share over the loud protests of Raymond, who maintained he was not entitled to one red cent.

During the days that followed, Raymond and Palmer traded threats and insults, with the older criminal usually getting the better of the young hothead.

On a long stretch of highway that had lulled everyone else to sleep, Clyde watched out of the corner of his eye as Raymond pulled his pistol from under his coat and pointed it at Palmer. With his left hand on the steering wheel, Clyde reached over the seat with his right and backhanded Raymond hard across the face.

Soon after that incident, Joe Palmer let Clyde know he needed a feather bed and decent grub if he was ever going to get back on his feet. Barrow understood and dropped him in front of a hotel in, of all places, Joplin, Missouri, promising to return for him in a month or six weeks.

Hilton Bybee had already taken his leave with his share of the bank loot. He lasted

The "new" Barrow Gang after the Eastham escape. *Left to right*: Clyde Barrow, Henry Methvin and Raymond Hamilton.

less than ten days on his own. Apprehended in Amarillo, he was back in Huntsville before he knew what had happened.

Clyde had Bonnie, so it was only natural that Raymond Hamilton wanted a female traveling companion, too. But when he showed up with Mary O'Dare at a Barrow family gathering on February 18, 1934, all in attendance did a double take. First of all, Mary was the wife of Raymond's incarcerated partner, Gene O'Dare, who had been put away for the next ninety-nine years. Second, she was a known prostitute with a sordid history of doing literally anything for money. And third, absolutely no one liked or trusted her. Even Floyd Hamilton, who as a rule thought his little brother could do no wrong, had a low opinion of Raymond's new girlfriend. He described Mary O'Dare as "a short girl with plenty of curves and a hard face covered by enough makeup to grow a crop."

Bonnie's hatred of Mary was surpassed only by her deep and abiding distrust of the conniving woman. From day one, she invoked and rigidly enforced a hard-and-fast rule that the latest addition to the gang was never allowed out of her sight under any circumstances. Clyde tolerated Mary's presence because he needed Raymond. Without him, bank jobs were out of the question. With him, top-dollar robberies went like clockwork and kept the money rolling in.

But it was only a matter of time until Raymond and Mary wore out their welcome. It started in late February after the lucrative looting of a bank in Lancaster near Dallas. Driving north toward Indiana, Clyde told Raymond to divide the $4,176 into four equal parts for Bonnie, Henry Methvin and the two of them. When Raymond spoke up on Mary's behalf, Clyde said the matter was not open to discussion.

Ever suspicious of Raymond, Clyde adjusted the rearview mirror so he could watch him count the money. Sure enough, Hamilton slipped a big wad of bills to Mary in violation of one of Clyde's cardinal rules. They could steal from the whole wide world, but they never ever stole from each other.

Less than a week later, the other shoe dropped. Bonnie came to Clyde with a story of betrayal that made his blood boil. Mary had approached her on the sly with a plan to drug the love of her life, take his bankroll and leave him high and dry. Mad as he was, Clyde gave Raymond Hamilton one last chance. He could stay if he came to his senses and dumped the double-crosser in the skirt. Raymond angrily refused and took off with Mary the next day.

Chapter 7

The End of the Road

Two weeks after the Eastham breakout, Lee Simmons was still at a loss as to how such an embarrassing escape could have happened on his watch. He had no plausible explanation for the rising chorus of critics that in his eyes looked more like a lynch mob with each passing day. The way the thin-skinned general manager of the state penal system saw it, the recent public pillorying of the Dallas County sheriff was a testimonial dinner compared to what the press and politicians were putting him through.

But the one question the beleaguered prison boss did not waste time thinking about was who to blame for the blow to his reputation. Lack of evidence be damned, it had to be Clyde Barrow, and he would get him no matter what.

That was the promise Simmons made to Major Crowson, the mortally wounded "high rider." Although doctors rated his chances of recovery at slim to none, Crowson hung on for eleven days. Before he died, he named Joe Palmer as his killer, saying he "didn't give me a dog's chance," and made Simmons swear he would to send him to the chair. The GM told him he could count on it, but his mind was on Clyde Barrow.

The one thing Simmons knew for certain was that local cops with their limited resources were no match for the Barrow Gang. It would take a group of experienced and ruthless lawmen capable of tracking Bonnie and Clyde and eliminating them once they had the fugitives in their sights. No capture, no arrest, just a shoot-to-kill execution.

Frank Hamer, the legendary Texas Ranger, was not Lee Simmons's first choice to lead the manhunt, and for good reason. He had to sell the governor on his idea of a no-quarter posse, and Miriam Ferguson detested Hamer as much as he despised her and her husband, Jim, the impeached ex-governor removed from office in 1917. After "Ma," Texas's first female chief executive, was elected to a second term in the fall of 1932, Hamer opted for early retirement rather than give Mrs. Ferguson the satisfaction of firing him in the housecleaning of the khaki corps that had been a key component of her campaign.

Before Simmons even brought Hamer's name up in his private meeting with the governor, he admitted that he had exhausted the short list of prospects. Two other qualified candidates had turned him down flat because the task entailed killing a woman. He left "Ma" Ferguson's office with a unique "Special Escape Investigator for the Texas Prison System" commission and sufficient funds for a manhunt that might take months.

Why was forty-nine-year-old Frank Hamer the only man for the job? With fifty-three confirmed kills in his thirty-year career, he was the most prolific killer in Texas history. Hamer had shot to death more men than John Wesley Hardin, Bill Longley, Ben Thompson, Clay Allison or any other gunfighter in the blood-soaked nineteenth century.

Hamer's philosophy was as chilling as it was simple. He liked to tell raw Ranger recruits, "We're here to enforce the law, and the best way is a .45 slug in the gut." And when it came to the "Texas brag," Hamer could make the most preposterous of claims with the straightest of faces. In an interview with the state's most respected historian, he actually stated that his superior eyesight made it possible for him to observe bullets from gun barrel to target.

Lee Simmons sat down with Frank Hamer at his home in Austin on February 10, 1934. The fate of Bonnie Parker was not a sticking point, but the "Special Escape Investigator" salary was. He was pulling down $500 a month with an oil company, nearly three times more than Simmons could afford to pay him. That was when the prison official played his hole card. Everything Hamer found on Bonnie and Clyde and in their vehicle—their clothing, personal possessions and arsenal—would be his and his alone. With true-crime collectibles a hot commodity in the 1930s, the old Ranger stood to make a small fortune. The way his eyes lit up told Simmons they had a deal.

As big believers in the importance of family, Clyde and Bonnie were willing to take Henry Methvin home whenever he wished. Their first trip to Bienville Parish, less than an hour's drive from Shreveport in northwest Louisiana, in February 1934 was a quick in-and-out, but the second after

A mug shot close-up of Henry Methvin, who put Bonnie and Clyde "on the spot." *From the collections of Texas/Dallas History and Archives Division, Dallas Public Library.*

the split with Raymond Hamilton in early March lasted several days. While Methvin visited with his kinfolks, the two weary Texans took it easy in an abandoned house that became their private retreat.

For someone whose chief survival skill was his gift for reading people, Clyde badly misjudged Henry and the Methvins, especially family patriarch Ivy. While the backwoods bumpkins always rolled out the red carpet for Bonnie and Clyde, bending over backward to make them feel safe and welcome, when their guests were not around they gave Henry hell for ever getting involved with America's most wanted couple. Ivy, in particular, hounded his son day and night to save his own skin by putting his new friends "on the spot." By the end of the March visit, Henry was ready to betray Clyde and Bonnie. He told his father to start the ball rolling and have everything ready to go the next time the trio came to visit.

Ivy Methvin reached out to Sheriff Henderson Jordan, who got in contact with Frank Hamer. The Methvin boy was prepared to play the Judas part in exchange for a full pardon. It took several weeks, but Hamer persevered until he had an official document signed by Lee Simmons and Governor Ferguson guaranteeing Henry Methvin a free pass.

Hamer was as pleased as Punch. He did not have to go to all the trouble of hunting his quarry down. Bonnie and Clyde's trusted sidekick would hand them to him on a silver platter.

Clyde, of course, had no way of knowing the deadly die had been cast. Yet his fatalistic mood at a gathering of the Barrows and Parkers suggested he sensed the end was fast approaching. In front of both families, he appealed to Bonnie to save herself before it was too late. She hobbled over to him on her bad leg, gave him a hug and said with a sad smile, "When my time comes, I want it to be with you."

No one can say for sure what Clyde, Bonnie and Henry Methvin were doing on a hilltop five miles from Grapevine on the morning of April 1, 1934. One theory is they were waiting for relatives to arrive for an Easter Sunday celebration. Another more sinister hypothesis is that Clyde selected the site because it was one of Raymond Hamilton's favorite hiding places, and he had made up his mind to finish off his former partner.

Bonnie was playing with a pet rabbit she planned to give her mother, Clyde was dozing in the backseat and Methvin, with BAR in hand, was watching the road. Henry's heart skipped a beat when two motorcycle-riding highway patrolmen cruised by, circled back and turned down the dirt road toward the outlaws.

Cool as a cucumber, Bonnie picked up the bunny and walked slowly to the car to wake Clyde. He rubbed his eyes and jumped out of the car holding a sawed-off shotgun behind his back. When the two-wheeled cops rolled to within ten yards of the car, he muttered under his breath to Methvin, "Let's take them."

What Clyde meant was to get the drop on the young highway patrolmen, both in their twenties, and take them hostage like the Barrow Gang had done to other unsuspecting "laws." But Methvin misunderstood and cut loose with the BAR, blowing the lead cop off his cycle. The second patrolman slid to a stop on the loose dirt and reached for the shotgun strapped to the rear fender of his motorcycle. Faced yet again with a "kill or be killed" dilemma, Clyde won the quick-draw contest with three blasts of man-killing buckshot.

An excited farmer was waiting next to the dead bodies when the authorities converged on the scene. He had quite a tale to tell, which happened to have no basis in fact. From a distance of several hundred yards, he claimed to have witnessed Bonnie Parker administer coups de grace to the wounded officers. He strained his credibility to the breaking point with the absurd assertion that both Raymond Hamilton and Bonnie's sister Billie were on hand for the double homicide.

The newspapers had a field day with the bizarre eyewitness account and transformed Bonnie overnight from a romantic interest along for the ride to a heartless executioner. Readers shed tears in their morning oatmeal at photographs of the fiancée of one highway patrolman attending his funeral in the wedding dress she would never wear.

The superintendent of the Texas highway patrol offered a $1,000 reward for "the dead bodies of the Grapevine slayers." Concerned that voters would not learn of her role in Frank Hamer's manhunt until after the fact, Governor Ferguson sweetened the reward with $500 for each killer, "dead or alive."

Joe Palmer had rejoined the gang before Grapevine but missed out on the Easter murders because of personal business in Dallas. He spent most of the month of April with Clyde, Bonnie and Henry Methvin and lent a hand in the May 3 robbery of an Iowa bank.

Clyde liked having Palmer around and invited him to come along for some rest and recreation at their Louisiana retreat. "We'll do some fishing," he said, painting a relaxing picture of a nearby lake. "We'll probably jump in and swim around a little."

But Louisiana was not far enough for Palmer, who believed they should go someplace where no one would be looking for them. "Why don't y'all come up north with me? Maybe go to that World's Fair in Chicago?"

Clyde would not hear of it. The Windy City was a two-day drive from Dallas, and he wanted to stay close to home and his mother regardless of the risk. When they dropped him off in Joplin, Joe Palmer must have wondered if he would ever see Clyde and Bonnie again.

On their way back from Missouri, the couple detoured through Dallas in order to snatch a few hours of quality time with their folks. While Clyde joked and kidded with his kin, his soul mate sat down with her mother for a serious heart-to-heart. Bonnie told Emma Parker that it was her wish to spend her final night at home, not in a funeral parlor. Horrified by the mere mention of her daughter's death, the woman became distraught and tried to change the subject. Bonnie patted her hand and said it was silly to stick her head in the sand. Then she gave her the poem she had just written. Bonnie called the sixteen stanzas "The End of the Line," but a newspaperman would change the title to "The Story of Bonnie and Clyde."

Two weeks later, on May 21, Clyde and Bonnie left Henry at the Methvin homestead en route to their hideaway in the woods. Henry Methvin told his father they were back and to notify the sheriff.

Later that day, Clyde picked up Henry and drove into Shreveport. He parked in front of a downtown café and sent the errand boy in for sandwiches. Methvin was standing at the counter waiting on his order when a passing police car activated Clyde's infallible alarm. He drove off, leaving Methvin, who had been taught what to do in those situations, to make it back to the hideaway as best he could.

Late that afternoon, Sheriff Henderson Jordan called Frank Hamer at the Shreveport motel, where he had spent the past week sitting by the telephone. "It's time," was all he said. The man-hunter and his recently organized posse loaded their weapons and headed for the spot the sheriff had selected for the ambush.

The gravel road was the only way in and out of the woods that concealed Clyde and Bonnie's not-so-secret hideout. Arriving at the location well after midnight, the Texans exchanged terse pleasantries with Sheriff Jordan and his right-hand man, Deputy Prentiss Oakley, and went to work constructing a "blind" out of tree limbs and brush.

Frank Hamer and Manny Gault (an old friend from his Ranger days), the two Dallas deputy sheriffs—Bob Alcorn and Ted Hinton—and the two Louisiana lawmen lay in wait with their guns at the ready the rest of that night and all the next day and night. When the sun broke the horizon on Wednesday, May 23, 1934, the six executioners were tired, hungry and covered with mosquito and tick bites from head to foot. As anxious as they were to get it over with, a healthy respect for Clyde Barrow's skill with a gun and a car kept their nerves on edge.

Since only the Dallas deputies had ever seen Clyde in the flesh, it fell to them to make the call. The distant rumble of the expensive V-8 Barrow had picked up weeks earlier in Topeka caught Alcorn and Hinton's attention. Several heartbeats later, the fast-moving V-8 topped the hill and started to slow down at the sight of Ivy Methvin's truck jacked up on the side of the road.

"This is him," Ted Hinton whispered in Bob Alcorn's ear. "This is it. It's Clyde."

Clyde instantly recognized Methvin's truck. He should have, since the generous bandit had bought it for him. He pulled alongside and asked the old man if he needed any help. Ivy Methvin shook his head violently, clutched his stomach and staggered into the woods as if to throw up.

Clyde was puzzled by this odd behavior but did not have the time to think about it with a timber truck coming down the hill toward him. He had to clear the lane. As he shifted gears and started to accelerate, Bonnie glanced over at Clyde and saw a man with a rifle rise up from a brush pile twenty feet to her lover's left. Five more armed figures suddenly materialized in the morning mist, and the firing squad was ready.

The bullet-riddled death car after the Louisiana ambush.

Bonnie's scream was drowned out by the sound of the first two gunshots, both of which struck Clyde in the head. Twenty-seven more bullets tore him to pieces, inflicting deadly damage throughout his upper body and severing his spinal cord. Bonnie was hit by at least twenty-eight shots, including one slug that came out the top of her head, knocking her red hat into the back seat. Two ripped through her face with a force that shattered her jaw and teeth, and a third blew the fingers off her tiny right hand.

As the four other lawmen kept blasting away with shotguns, Alcorn and Hinton ran after the slow-motion death car, firing into the trunk with their pistols. The shooting did not cease until the Ford finally rolled off the road and into a ditch.

Ted Hinton reached the bullet-riddled car first. He tried to pull the driver's side door open, but it was wedged tight against the ditch. There is no need to speculate about what he did next and, more importantly, what he saw. We have Hinton's own words, as dictated to a freelance writer for the book *Ambush*, published a year and a half after his death in 1977:

> *I scramble over the hood of the car and throw open the door on Bonnie's side. The impression will linger with me from this instant—I see her falling out of the opened door, a beautiful and petite young girl who is soft and warm, with hair carefully fixed, and I smell a light perfume against the burned-cordite smell of gunpowder, the sweet and unreal smell of blood.*

I stand her up, full standing, a tiny frail girl she seems now, and I cannot believe that I do not really feel her breathing, but I look into her face and I see that she is dead.

What he did and what he saw on May 23, 1934, haunted Ted Hinton for the rest of his days. Clearly he felt something—was it love?—for the flirtatious waitress who had brought him coffee in the downtown Dallas café before Clyde Barrow entered her life. Now that secret affection mixed with a heaping helping of guilt would gnaw at him for the next thirty-three years.

Chapter 8
Big Send-off in Big D

Frank Hamer was far more interested in the contents of the trunk than the two dead bodies in the front seat. Before the smoke had even cleared, the ex-Ranger with dollar signs dancing in his head got busy inventorying his take.

Try as he may, Hamer did not succeed in seizing every item of value. When he was not looking, Bob Alcorn slipped Clyde's saxophone, one of the outlaw's prize possessions, under his coat. The Dallas deputy did not hold onto it for long, however, and a little while later quietly presented the musical instrument to the Barrow family. The suitcase of cash Clyde was known to have been carrying the day he died also vanished. No one ever owned up to taking it, but Sheriff Henderson Jordan's unexpected purchase of an auction barn and a sizeable parcel of land soon after the ambush made him the likely candidate.

With his loot safe and secure, Hamer declared the next order of business was to tell the world what they had done. Leaving Alcorn and Manny Gault behind to keep an eye on the death car and the bodies, Hamer and the three other possemen drove to the closest town to look for a pay phone. Locating a phone booth at a gas station in tiny Gibsland, a hamlet of fewer than one thousand, Sheriff Jordan went first, placing a call to the Bienville Parish coroner. He explained to J.L. Wade why and where his services were required and told him not to forget to bring a tow truck. Next it was Ted Hinton's turn, and the deputy dutifully dialed his superior in Dallas. Sheriff Smoot Schmid was overjoyed by the news of Bonnie and Clyde's demise and informed Hinton he was on his way to Louisiana to share the spotlight. Hamer went last. His conversation with Lee Simmons was brief and to the point. When the prison boss came on the line, he uttered the classic understatement: "Well, we got them."

The lawmen were so immersed in their telephone conversations that they were oblivious to the crowd of eavesdroppers listening to their every word. When it came time to drive back to the scene of the slaughter, a long line of cars was waiting to tail them.

The quartet arrived at the ambush site to find it crawling with souvenir hunters. Even though Alcorn and Gault were on the verge of being overrun, they stopped one man from severing Clyde's ear and another from removing his trigger finger. But when their backs were turned, someone took a pair of scissors to Bonnie's gore-caked hair and dress. It was a carnival of out-of-control ghouls.

Again at full strength, the six-man posse cleared a path through the mob for the coroner and the tow truck. In the time it took for the wrecker driver to hook up the Ford, J.L Wade stated the obvious: the cause of death for both occupants was multiple gunshot wounds. Less than ten minutes later, the tow truck and the two carloads of snipers started rolling toward Arcadia, followed by a caravan of two hundred private vehicles.

The sleepy town of three thousand had mushroomed into a madhouse of sixteen thousand frenzied curiosity seekers, with each and every one jockeying for a front-row seat. To make a bad situation much worse, the wrecker broke down in front of the school at the very moment the students went outside for recess. Students swarmed the death car for a peek at the slain strangers and got more than their young minds could handle when a girl pulled back the sheet covering Bonnie's face and torso. The horrible sight provoked a chorus of screams and sent many of the kids scampering for the safety of their classrooms.

A relief wrecker towed the death car to the city impound lot, where a high fence kept the mob at bay. The bodies were lifted onto stretchers and carried to the back room of a furniture store, which doubled as the morgue. Free at last from the prying eyes of the public, Coroner Wade conducted a complete postmortem. Newspaper photographers, who had taken shots of Bonnie and Clyde on the street through the shattered windows of the death car, were barred from the autopsy. It was the decent thing to do. But shortly after the coroner finished his grisly chore, a photographer either snuck into the room or was given access by somebody in authority. And that was how pictures of the naked bodies of Bonnie and Clyde landed on the front pages of newspapers from coast to coast.

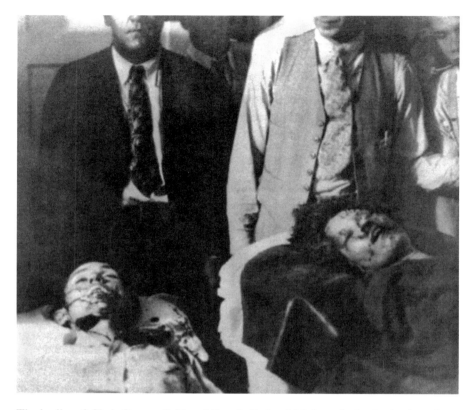

The bodies of Clyde Barrow (left) and Bonnie Parker (right) on display in the Arcadia morgue.

As if that was not sordid enough, Frank Hamer took it upon himself to turn the autopsy into a public spectacle. Once the bodies were covered up to the neck, he ordered the local cops to let everybody in. That was too much for a coroner's assistant, who watched over the remains and sprayed embalming fluid on anybody who got too close.

Looking like a party of overdressed deer hunters, the six shooters posed for a group picture. The other five responded to reporters' questions with a silent shake of the head or a gruff "no comment," but Hamer was happy to oblige. He repeated the lie he had told Lee Simmons on the phone that "both Clyde and Bonnie reached for their guns," leaving the posse with no choice but to annihilate them. Hamer hastened to add with a hangdog expression that he had "hated to bust a cap on a woman," conveniently omitting the fact that he fired the last rounds into Bonnie to make sure she was good and dead.

Accompanied by his eldest child, Jack, Henry Barrow arrived in Arcadia in the middle of the afternoon to claim his boy's body. The grieving father told the assassins what they wanted to hear: that they were only doing their job and he did not blame them for Clyde's violent end.

Barrow presumed Henry Methvin had died along with Clyde and Bonnie and was startled to learn their constant companion was very much alive and as free as a bird. Henry Barrow may have been an illiterate farmer, but he was nobody's fool. It was clear to him Henry Methvin had Clyde's blood on his hands.

Overnight, the bodies were transported to two different funeral homes in Dallas. Emma Parker would break every promise she had made to her daughter. She insisted on separate funerals and separate burials in spite of Bonnie's desire to spend eternity alongside the love of her life. In their last meeting, Bonnie had begged her not to bad-mouth Clyde after she was gone, but it was not in the domineering woman's nature to hold her tongue. Trembling with rage, Emma Parker said for publication, "He had her for two years. Look what it got her. He's not going to have her anymore. She's mine now."

The last thing the *Morning News* wanted to see was a repetition of the 1925 send-off for an executed bootlegger. Sidney "Pete" Welk was a well-known and well-liked seller of illegal spirits in those Prohibition days convicted of killing a deputy sheriff in an attempted escape from the Dallas County jail. As yet, no white man had been electrocuted in the state's newfangled chair, and many Dallasites objected strenuously to Welk being the first. To the horror of the business community and the well-to-do, a throng ten thousand strong showed up at the jam-packed cemetery to tell old Pete goodbye.

On Thursday, May 24, 1934, the day visitations were scheduled at the funeral homes, an editorial in the *Morning News* implored readers to behave themselves. "The community owes a debt to itself and to posterity to see to it, by injunction if need be, that no show is made of the interment of the brutal pair who have met a fate that they deserved."

The Sparkman-Holtz-Brand Chapel had planned on a private viewing of Clyde's open casket for the family and a preapproved list of friends only. But one look at the rowdy crowd outside caused the funeral home director to change his mind. "Otherwise, we'll never get them to disperse," he explained. "They've torn up all my shrubbery, all my lawn."

All day Thursday and late into the night, people stood in a long line around the block for a glimpse of the West Dallas desperado. Many were morbid, while some were drunk and cracking crude jokes. After repeated requests from the Barrows, the police finally intervened and restored a semblance of dignified order. The public viewing resumed bright and early Friday and ended only with the memorial service that afternoon. No one tried to keep count, but the best guess of the funeral home staff was that upward of thirty thousand filed past Clyde Barrow's coffin.

So much for the editorial admonishment of the *Dallas Morning News*.

All that kept the burial from getting out of control was its brevity. Clyde was lowered into an extra-wide grave next to Buck, as the minister shouted a few words over the din of the multitude. From a small plane circling overhead, a remembrance bouquet was dropped to the ground below, setting off a wild scramble for the flowers. Rumor had it that the floral tribute was paid for by gambler Benny Binion, the future Las Vegas icon.

Lost in the crowd was a face familiar to every cop in the Southwest. With Clyde Barrow and Bonnie Parker stricken from the most-wanted list, Joe Palmer had taken their place. Nonetheless, he risked capture or worse to pay his last respects to his departed friends and partners in crime. They had always done right by him, and it was the least he could do for them.

Emma Parker pushed Bonnie's funeral back to Saturday in order not to conflict with Clyde's. She did so not out of consideration for the Barrows but to maximize the turnout at her own child's services. The visitation for Bonnie at McKamy-Campbell Funeral Home was a sedate affair compared to the near-riot at the viewing for her companion in love and crime. Emma dressed her daughter in a blue silk negligee, a scandalously inappropriate choice for the solemn occasion, and partially concealed her mutilated face with a translucent white veil. She later claimed twenty thousand people came by for one last look, but more objective observers discounted that ego-inflated figure as too high by half.

Emma Parker boycotted the Friday funeral for Clyde. The Barrows could have retaliated in kind but instead chose to show more class and compassion than the woman who had always looked down on them. Besides, the funeral was for Bonnie, not her mother, and all of Clyde's kin wanted to bid her farewell. Clearly unprepared for the sight of so many Barrows, Emma backpedaled a bit and at the last moment asked L.C. to serve as one of the six pallbearers.

Bonnie's sister Billie came to the funeral in chains, surrounded by a detail of Texas Rangers and Tarrant County deputy sheriffs. She was still being held in the Fort Worth jail on trumped-up charges stemming from the Easter shootings of the two motorcycle patrolmen. Escorted under armed guard to the front of the chapel, Billie fainted at the sight of her sibling's disfigured face.

The huge crowd outside the funeral home for Bonnie's "visitation."

Pallbearers carry Bonnie's casket down the steps from the funeral home.

The marker on the grave of Bonnie Parker.

Attended by 150 relatives and friends, the memorial service was closed to the public. The 300 spectators who waited outside the chapel were on their best behavior due in part to stern warnings from a small army of police officers under orders to prevent a repeat of the raucous scene the previous day. When the doors opened and the pallbearers emerged with the casket on their shoulders, the obedient crowd parted like the biblical Red Sea.

Bonnie was laid to rest in Fish Trap Cemetery right next to a pair of miniature graves containing Billie's two young children, who had died suddenly from food poisoning the previous year. Bonnie Parker was not alone, but she would never get her wish to spend eternity close to Clyde.

Chapter 9

Rubbing Salt in the Wound

With Clyde and Bonnie dead and gone, everyone struggled to get on with their lives as best they could. It was hardest for the immediate families and closest friends, whose unbearable burden of grief was not lightened in the least by the inevitability of a violent end for the cursed couple. Many other Dallasites who had never come into contact with the infamous outlaws or their home base in West Dallas were upset by the extreme methods employed to end their crime spree and the vicious, premeditated murder of a female.

Initially, the Dallas County sheriff brooded over missing out on the ambush and the bounty of benefits certain to come with being a member of the posse. First, there was the reward, expected to total in the thousands of dollars. But after a number of businesses and wealthy individuals reneged on their cash commitments, Smoot Schmid's two deputies pocketed checks in the amount of $200.23. Second, there was the public backlash. Strong feelings against Frank Hamer and his hit squad percolated up the social ladder from the West End to the affluent elite. A well-read newspaper columnist reported hearing denunciations of the Bonnie and Clyde killing in an exclusive country club. Schmid witnessed firsthand how Bob Alcorn and Ted Hinton were snubbed by erstwhile friends and criticized to their faces for taking part in the ambush. When it was all said and done, the sheriff considered himself fortunate to have not been among the triggermen.

Although the final curtain had not yet dropped on the subordinate dramas of Raymond Hamilton and other Barrow Gang associates, Dallas in general and the Barrows and Parkers in particular took comfort in the belief that the worst was behind them. But that was before the government decided to make an example of everybody who ever had anything to do with Bonnie and Clyde.

At a standing-room-only press conference in late 1934, U.S. Attorney Clyde Eastus unveiled his plan to pursue "aiding and abetting" prosecution under a new law that made it a crime punishable by up to two years imprisonment to "harbor" a federal fugitive. Formal charges were filed, and two dozen defendants were rounded up.

How the U.S. attorney went about picking and choosing those to try and those to pass over mystified all concerned. The mothers of Clyde, Bonnie and Raymond Hamilton were thrown into jail, as were Clyde's brother L.C., his teenage sister Marie and her husband, Joe Bill Francis, as well as Bonnie's sister Billie Jean. Family members avoiding prosecution included Henry Barrow, Jack his oldest son, sisters Artie and Nell and Buster Parker, Bonnie's brother. Among those defendants not related by blood to the three clans were W.D. Jones, Hilton Bybee, Henry Methvin, Mary O'Dare, James Mullen and Blanche Barrow, who the feds went to the trouble and expense to bring to Texas from her Missouri prison cell.

Separate trials for the sexes were scheduled for the last week of February 1935. The accused were taken to and from the federal courthouse by paddy wagon. The women could have been mistaken for red-eyed spectators, but there was no question about the men, who came to court in leg irons, handcuffs and chains wrapped around their necks. L.C. Barrow's chain-mate was none other than Henry Methvin, and it was all he could do to keep from throttling the snake-in-the-grass who had set his brother up for the kill.

In his opening statement, U.S. Attorney Eastus ventured to say that if George Washington had known that people such as those in the docket would wind up in America, he would have thought twice about crossing the Delaware. It was that kind of theatrical trial.

Because of her weakened condition, made all the worse by a month of confinement, Cumie Barrow had to be carried into the courtroom in a chair. On the stand, she refused to apologize for seeing Clyde wherever and whenever possible and reaffirmed her unconditional love for her dead son.

Twenty defendants stood trial, and twenty were found guilty by plea or by jury verdict. Judge W.H. Atwell, himself a former U.S. attorney, exercised judicial discretion in assessing the penalties rather than imposing a one-size-fits-all punishment. Atwell also gave the proceedings the human touch with his often-lengthy exchanges with the defendants. In the case of Cumie

Female defendants at the "harboring" trial.

After the deaths of two sons and a month in jail, Cumie Barrow had to be carried into the "harboring" trial. *From the collections of Texas/Dallas History and Archives Division, Dallas Public Library.*

Barrow, he asked the sixty-year-old mother, "What sentence do you think you should receive?"

"I think thirty more days would be right," she replied.

"How about sixty days?" was the judge's counter-offer.

Cumie's expression did not change as she sighed, "Well, it's up to you, Judge."

"Well, I want to do what's right," continued Atwell in his own defense. "You know what you've done, and so do I."

Sensing he might be softening, Cumie added plaintively, "My health's rather bad, Judge."

"All right. Thirty days then."

To keep it fair and uniform, Atwell also gave Bonnie's and Raymond Hamilton's mothers one more month behind bars.

Marie Barrow took the prize for the lightest sentence—one hour in police custody—and was home in time for dinner. Two-year maximums went to W.D. Jones and Floyd Hamilton, but to the brother of the notorious Raymond, Judge Atwell remarked, "If you ever need a friend, write to me."

For those defendants like W.D., Blanche and Bybee already in stir, their sentences were purely symbolic. Judge Atwell ruled the "harboring" terms could be served concurrently, thereby adding not a single day to their time behind bars.

"The United States Attorney's office and the Department of Justice bureau of investigation is very pleased with the conviction of these persons," Prosecutor Eastus gloated from the steps of the federal courthouse. "We feel that the result will have a wholesome effect on others who are harboring or concealing persons wanted by the government."

In Dallas and the rest of the country, the "harboring" trial did not receive rave reviews. The prosecution of the three mothers and other relatives and friends with no criminal record was seen by a significant portion of the public as rubbing salt in the wound. That was how Deputy Ted Hinton saw it. "I didn't think it was right at all" was his parting comment on the subject in his posthumously published book. When the U.S. marshal asked him to escort several of the sentenced to their penal destinations, he politely but firmly declined.

The "harboring" trial closed the book on Bonnie and Clyde. The surviving characters were now free to add their personal postscripts.

With the money he made from the sale of the gas station in 1940, Henry Barrow could afford a special treat for his wife of half a century: a home with indoor plumbing. But due to the agonizing ordeal she had endured over the deaths of Buck and Clyde, Cumie's health continued to decline until her

Baby sister Marie ended up with the third-longest rap sheet in the Barrow family. *RGD5f952 Houston Public Library HMRC.*

passing in 1942 at the age of sixty-seven. Her husband hung on for fifteen more years before dying at eighty-three in 1957. The Barrows were buried where they belonged: next to their sons' common plot.

Of the remaining children, only Nell and Artie succeeded in staying out of trouble. They lived quietly and far from the headlines until their deaths in 1968 and 1981, respectively.

Their baby sister was a different story. Marie was in and out of jail well into her thirties, and one of her incarcerations was responsible for her missing her mother's funeral. In her old age, Marie survived off the sale of Clyde's miscellaneous keepsakes on the memorabilia market. She died a year shy of the twenty-first century at the age of eighty-one.

Elvin "Jack" Barrow did everything short of changing his name to live down the notoriety of Clyde and Buck. He relished the role of the "respectable" Barrow until one night in 1939, when he killed a man in a barroom brawl. A better lawyer might have gotten him off on self-defense, but he wound up spending time in the joint like his two disreputable brothers. Jack celebrated only fifty-two birthdays before preceding his father in death by five years.

L.C., the youngest boy, worshipped Clyde until his dying day. After prolonged bouts with drugs and alcohol that had a lot to do with prison terms for forgery and theft, he straightened out and drove trucks for a living. Even in his later years, the mere mention of Clyde's name brought tears to his eyes. L.C. was sixty-six when he died in 1979.

As for the Parkers, Emma was never the same after Bonnie's death. She lost interest in life and died a decade later at fifty-seven. Buster, the brother, drank himself into an early grave at fifty-six, leaving sister Billie Jean to raise his little girl, Bonnie. Billie Jean was the champion survivor of the Parkers, reaching the age of eighty before her departure in 1993.

Frank Hamer maintained a low public profile for the rest of his life, which came to a close in 1955. The booty from the ambush helped to pay for a comfortable retirement and made unnecessary a tell-all book that would have subjected the killing of Bonnie and Clyde to unwanted scrutiny.

Three years after the ambush, Manny Gault was accepted back into the good graces of the Texas Rangers. He died a decade later in 1947.

Henderson Jordan, the Louisiana sheriff, held on with all his might to the 1934 Ford Deluxe Sedan that took Bonnie and Clyde on their last ride. But the legal owner in Kansas demanded it back with the 160-plus bullet holes and all the bloodstains, and a judge ruled she was entitled to the macabre mess. Jordan vacated his office at the end of his second term in 1940, and eighteen years later at age sixty-one, he was killed instantly in a head-on highway collision.

Chief Deputy Prentiss Oakley succeeded Jordan as sheriff. He was not shy about admitting to anybody who would listen that he fired the first shot at Bonnie and Clyde and they were not given a chance to surrender. Oakley was in his early fifties when he died of natural causes a year before his old boss.

Before that fateful morning in the Louisiana woods, Bob Alcorn and Ted Hinton believed they would always be remembered as two of the six who took Clyde Barrow and Bonnie Parker off the street. They never dreamed the ambush would be an indelible stain on their reputations instead of a badge of honor. Both ran for Smoot Schmid's job after he retired, but the voters did not want a sheriff with so much blood on his hands. Alcorn quit law enforcement and died on the thirtieth anniversary of the ambush in 1964. Hinton spent much of his free time with the Barrows acting as their quasi-official press agent and trying to make amends for gunning down Clyde. He was the last living member of the posse at the time of his death in 1977.

Roy Thornton, Bonnie's lawfully wedded husband, must not have had a jealous bone in his body. When informed of the ambush, he was quoted

The toll taken by drugs and drinking shows in this 1949 photo of W.D. Jones. *RGD5f6410 Houston Public Library HMRC.*

as saying he was happy they went down together. Three years later, in 1937, he tried his own rash escape from the Eastham farm and died in the attempt.

After serving long prison stretches in Texas and Mississippi, Ralph Fults started over from scratch in the late 1940s. Marriage to a loving woman gave the once-incorrigible character the strength to straighten up and fly right, enabling him to stay out of jail. For a career criminal with an epic rap sheet, his eighty-two-year lifespan bordered on the unbelievable.

Drugs and alcohol were the twin banes of W.D. Jones's existence after his release from prison. He spent the rest of his life in the Houston area, where in 1974 he was shotgunned to death by a jealous husband or boyfriend after a long night of boozing.

Henry Methvin did not take full advantage of his deal with Texas authorities. He was working a straight job near Lake Charles, Louisiana, in 1948, when one of two things happened: either he got drunk and fell asleep on the railroad tracks, a strange spot to take a nap, or he was knocked unconscious and placed in the path of an oncoming train that sliced him clean in two.

Last but far from least, there was Buck's widow, Blanche. A model prisoner in Missouri, she was turned loose in 1939 and went straight back to Dallas, where she married and settled into the quiet life of a housewife. Her angry objection to the 1967 motion picture *Bonnie and Clyde* was that Estelle Parson's Academy Award–winning portrayal "made me look like a screaming horse's ass." Blanche was seventy-seven years old when cancer came for her in 1988.

Bonnie Parker still speaks to the world nearly eighty years after her death. Here in its entirety is "The End of the Line."

You've read the story of Jesse James—
Of how he lived and died;
If you're still in need
Of something to read
Here's the story of Bonnie and Clyde.

Now Bonnie and Clyde are the Barrow gang
I'm sure you all have read
How they rob and steal
And those who squeal
Are usually found dying or dead.

There's lots of untruths in those write-ups;
They're not so ruthless as that;
Their nature is raw;
They hate the law—
The stool pigeons, spotters and rats.

They call them cold-blooded killers;
They say they are heartless and mean;
But I say this with pride,
That I once knew Clyde
When he was honest and upright and clean.

But the laws fooled around,
Kept taking him down
And locking him up in a cell,
Till he said to me,
"I'll never be free,
So I'll meet a few of them in hell."

The road was dimly lighted;
There were no highway signs to guide;
But they made up their minds
If all roads were blind,
They wouldn't give up till they died.

The road gets dimmer and dimmer;
Sometimes you can hardly see;
But it's fight, man to man,
And do all you can,
For they know they can never be free.

From heart-break some people have suffered;
From weariness some people have died;
But take all in all,
Our troubles are small
Till we get like Bonnie and Clyde.

If a policeman is killed in Dallas,
And they have no clue or guide;
If they can't find a fiend,
They just wipe their slate clean
And hang it on Bonnie and Clyde.

There's two crimes committed in America,
Not accredited to the Barrow mob;
They had no hand
In the kidnap demand,
Nor the Kansas City Depot job.

A newsboy once said to his buddy:
"I wish old Clyde would get jumped;
In these awful times
We'd make a few dimes
If five or six cops would get bumped."

The police haven't got the report yet
But Clyde called me up today;
He said, "Don't start any fights—
We aren't working nights—
We're joining the NRA."

From Irving to the West Dallas viaduct
Is known as the Great Divide,
Where the women are kin,
And the men are men,
And they won't "stool" on Bonnie and Clyde.

If they try to act like citizens
And rent them a nice little flat,
About the third night
They're invited to fight
By a sub-gun's rat-tat-tat.

They don't think they're too smart or desperate,
They know the law always wins;
They've been shot at before,
But they do not ignore
That death is the wages of sin.

Some day they'll go down together;
And they'll bury them side by side,
To a few it'll be grief—
To the law a relief—
But it's death for Bonnie and Clyde.

Chapter 10

The Brothers Hamilton

Following the March 6, 1934 split with Clyde and Bonnie, Raymond Hamilton and his traveling companion, Mary O'Dare, made themselves scarce in the Panhandle of Texas, where the papers and the people paid little attention to current events in the eastern two-thirds of the sprawling state. But the Easter shooting of the two highway patrolmen in Grapevine made the news all the way out in Amarillo, as did the inaccurate eyewitness account of Raymond Hamilton as one of the cold-blooded killers.

For Raymond, it looked like Hillsboro all over again. He had been in Michigan when John Bucher was murdered, but the law had not let that stand in the way of pinning the rap on him. Before he let them blame him for another homicide someone else committed, he would speak out and set the record straight.

Raymond waited until he had driven clear across Texas before putting pen to paper. In a New Orleans hotel room, he sat down and wrote to a Dallas defense attorney who had represented him in the past: "I haven't been with Clyde Barrow since the Lancaster bank robbery. I want you to let the public and the whole world know I am not with Clyde Barrow, and don't go his speed. I'm a lone man and intend to stay that way." To authenticate the letter, Raymond rolled a finger across an ink pad and pressed the unique print below his signature.

The *Dallas Morning News* ran the letter on page one of the April 9, 1934 edition. Seventeen days later, the paper had an even bigger story to report: the capture of Raymond Hamilton.

Raymond was down to his last dollar and desperate to replenish his coffers. With a first-time accomplice stationed at the curb with the engine idling, Hamilton pulled a solo stickup of a bank in Lewisville north of Dallas on April 25. The robbery came off without a hitch but not the getaway. Cornered by the local cops, Raymond called it quits. "Don't shoot, boys," the smiling bandit shouted. "I'm fresh out of guns, ammo, whiskey and women."

A few days after taking up temporary residency in the Dallas jail, Raymond tore open a letter from Clyde:

> *I'm very sorry to hear of your getting captured, but due to the fact you offered no resistance, sympathy is lacking. The most I can do is hope you miss the "chair." The purpose of this letter is to remind you of all the "dirty deals" you have pulled. When I came to the farm after you I thought maybe the "joint" had changed you from a boastful punk. However, I learned too soon the mistake I had made.*
>
> *I don't claim to be too smart. I know that some day they will get me but it won't be without resistance.*

It took three trials in rapid succession, but frustrated prosecutors finally found a jury willing to give the handsome young defendant the death penalty. As Raymond shuffled in chains from the Walker County courtroom for the four-block ride to "Death Row," he saw Harry McCormick, the courageous reporter with the *Houston Press*, the muckraking tabloid that kept the *Chronicle* and the *Post* on their toes. For years, the investigative journalist had exposed the inhumane conditions and systematic mistreatment of inmates in Texas prisons.

"I'll break out of the death house," Raymond predicted with his usual bravado. "When I do, I'll come by to see you."

On June 29, 1934, Joe Palmer joined Raymond Hamilton in the cellblock of the central unit reserved for condemned prisoners. Minutes earlier, another Walker County jury had sentenced him to die for the murder of the high rider in the Eastham escape. When he was permitted to speak before the twelve men good and true retired to decide his fate, Palmer did not grovel or beg for mercy but instead proudly confessed to plugging the guard. "No power on earth could have kept me from killing [Major] Crowson. I hated him and meant to kill him if it was the last thing I ever did."

However, before the state got around to strapping them in "Old Sparky," Hamilton and Palmer escaped from Death Row. The first-of-its-kind breakout

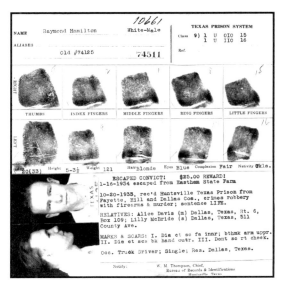

Raymond Hamilton's processing form from Eastham prison farm.

was conceived and carried out by an escape artist named Charlie Frazier, who in a period of sixteen years had busted out of three southern penitentiaries an amazing total of nine times.

In those days, underpaid prison guards supplemented their meager income by smuggling contraband to convicts. Anything could be had for a price—even three loaded pistols, as Charlie Frazier proved on a Sunday afternoon in July 1934.

After seizing control of Death Row, Frazier unlocked the cells of four fellow prisoners, including Joe Palmer but not Raymond Hamilton. For reasons that defied logic then and now, Palmer coaxed Frazier into taking along the baby-faced blond who had tried to shoot him in his sleep in the back seat of Clyde Barrow's car.

Firing wildly at the guard towers, the six men sprinted across the open courtyard to the final barrier. Three never made it, but Palmer, Hamilton and Blackie Thompson scaled the high wall and roared off in a waiting car driven by one of the two sisters who had handled all the arrangements for their friend Frazier.

If not for bad luck, poor Joe Palmer would have had no luck at all, and by early August, he was back on Death Row. Blackie Thompson perished in a gun battle with Amarillo police in December, the same month Raymond Hamilton came up for air. Hamilton robbed a warehouse near Dallas and went back into hiding.

Texans scanned their daily papers for the latest developments in the search for the fugitive nicknamed "the swashbuckling bandit king." For three months, he provided readers with thrills aplenty as he led lawmen on a wild five-state chase.

Older brother Floyd threw in with Raymond sometime that autumn, and together they robbed an East Texas bank in February 1935. Seeking sanctuary on their old home turf, the Hamiltons stumbled into half a dozen detectives in West Dallas but miraculously shot their way out of the trap.

Fleeing south to Beaumont, the brothers restocked their private arsenal by helping themselves to the contents of a federal armory. Plans to lay low in the North Texas countryside were spoiled outside McKinney, where they again vanished without a trace following a fierce gunfight.

The Hamiltons finally parted company at Raymond's insistence. His big brother had always looked out for him, and now it was his turn. Acutely aware they could end up like Clyde and Bonnie, cut to pieces by a posse with orders to shoot to kill, he wanted to spare Floyd such a grisly fate.

During her last month in office, Miriam Ferguson granted Ralph Fults a conditional pardon. The outgoing governor gave him the good news in person on a January 1935 visit to the Sugarland prison farm outside Houston. "Don't you do us like Buck did," said "Ma." Don't get caught up in that outlaw life again."

But Fults was not good at breaking bad habits and most times did not bother to try. After a couple weeks of going it alone on the outside, he decided beggars really could not be choosers and joined Raymond Hamilton, filling the opening left by his brother.

The resourceful sisters who had made the Death Row escape happen

A standing mug shot of Floyd Hamilton in his bib overalls. *From the collections of Texas/Dallas History and Archives Division, Dallas Public Library.*

arranged Raymond's March 18, 1935 meeting with Harry McCormick. The reporter had his hunches but did not know for a fact who would be waiting at the end of all the twists and turns through the streets of Houston until he opened a car door and saw a familiar grin.

"Hello, Harry," drawled Hamilton. "I'm sorry it took me so long to get here to talk to you, but when your life is on the line, you have to be mighty careful." The fugitive went on to praise the newspaperman for his crusade "to get humane treatment for the boys in 'the joint.'"

When it was McCormick's turn to a pose a question, he asked, "How did you manage that death cell break?"

Investigative reporter Harry McCormick risked his life to expose prison abuse. *RGD5f7483 Houston Public Library HMRC.*

"Well, of course, I got all the credit for that," Raymond said with a shrug, "but to tell the truth, I had very little to do with that escape. It was Charlie's baby all the way, and now I'm out, and he's rotting in that hole."

After explaining the debt he owed Joe Palmer for "putting in a good word for me" with Charlie Frazier, Raymond handed McCormick a grocery sack full of money. "Me and Ralph want you to give this to Joe's lawyer. We hope it'll buy a stay of execution."

A jittery Fults announced it was time to go. "To keep the feds off of you," Raymond told the reporter, "we best make out like we kidnapped you and held you against your will." The two fugitives left Harry McCormick bound and gagged in his own car and drove away in the darkness with their two crackerjack accomplices.

Hamilton and Fults parted on amicable terms later that month, leaving Raymond to keep on running all alone. He ducked into a Fort Worth railroad yard on April 5, 1935, for some much-needed shut-eye. He had just dozed off when a Dallas deputy sheriff stuck a six-gun in his ribs and barked, "Hoist 'em, Ray!"

To minimize the risk of another escape by Raymond Hamilton and Joe Palmer, their executions were fast-tracked for May 5, 1935. The execution of Raymond as a "habitual criminal" rather than for a specific capital offense offended many Texans' sense of right and wrong. A statewide petition drive to have his sentence commuted to life imprisonment gathered thousands of signatures, but the new governor refused to be swayed.

"This is as close to the electric chair as I'll ever be," Raymond bragged over breakfast on the appointed day. But his brave front cracked upon learning that Governor Allred had turned down his plea for executive clemency.

Later that afternoon, Raymond's lawyer told him all legal options had been exhausted. As the sun went down, he muttered to a guard, "I've got mighty little hope left."

Joe Palmer was the first to go. He shook Raymond's hand and said, "Goodbye, old pal. We're going to be happy in a few minutes. We'll meet on the other side." Then he turned and marched ramrod straight through the dreaded green door, greeting prison officials and spectators with a cheerful, "Good morning, gentlemen."

Raymond followed four minutes later. He entered the death chamber noticeably pale but smiling as always. He wished the priest at his side well on an upcoming trip to Ireland and took his seat. Once the leather mask, straps and connections were in place, the guards backed a safe distance away from the electric chair. Hidden behind a white curtain, the faceless executioner threw the switch. The dynamo whined as the current coursed through Raymond, causing his body to stiffen against the thick restraints. Two jolts later, the doctor pronounced him legally dead.

Floyd Hamilton was in the federal penitentiary at Leavenworth, serving his two years for "harboring," when word came of Raymond's execution. He could have turned over a new law-abiding leaf but chose instead to follow in his dead brother's footsteps.

Not long after leaving Leavenworth, Floyd took off on a wild bank-robbing binge across the Midwest. Apprehended in the summer of 1938, he signed off on a plea bargain that was supposed to send him to the slammer for less than a decade. But the judge tore up the agreement and shipped him off to escape-proof Alcatraz for thirty years.

On the morning of April 14, 1943, Floyd was working in the prison mat shop with Freddie Hunter, an associate of the notorious Alvin "Creepy" Karpis, and fellow bank robbers James Boarman and Harold Brest. The four overpowered the lone guard, jumped the captain on his rounds and tied both up before proceeding with their plan. In the interest of time, the inmates already had sawed the bars in two on the outside window. It took only seconds to remove the metal rods and slide through the opening a plank long enough to reach the perimeter fence.

Floyd went first, crawling on his hands and knees to the fence, where he dropped to the ground and began a careful descent down the steep cliff. One by one, his companions followed until the group reassembled at the edge of the ice-cold water. They stripped to their underwear, smeared grease on their bodies for insulation and started swimming across San Francisco Bay. By this time, the captain had worked his gag loose, but his shouts could not be heard over the noise of the woodshop. Eventually, he sounded the alarm with a whistle he snatched with his teeth from the guard's pocket.

The marksman in the roof tower spotted the four escapees in the water and opened fire in accordance with Alcatraz's unwritten shoot-to-kill policy. Brest was hit in the elbow, and Boarman died instantly from a bullet through the head. The wounded convict treaded water until dragged aboard a launch, but the dead body of his comrade sank beneath the waves, never to be recovered.

Hamilton and Hunter swam underwater back to "The Rock" and took cover in a cave. Guards flushed out Hunter within a few hours but did not think to look under a pile of debris, where the fourth prisoner was playing possum.

Floyd spent two wretched days and three miserable nights waiting to be found, but search parties never reexamined the cave. Half starved, badly dehydrated and bleeding from hundreds of abrasions, he retraced his route to the mat shop, where a startled guard discovered him fast asleep the next morning.

After fifteen more years, most of it spent in solitary, Floyd finally returned to the free world in 1958. For want of a better place, he wandered back to Dallas, where, much to his surprise, former deputy Ted Hinton and the current sheriff found him a job with a car dealer. He proved to be the perfect employee, showing up for work every day until his retirement.

Floyd Hamilton outlived the brother he loved more than life itself by forty-nine years. The old outlaw faced his death in 1984 with the serenity that came with the conviction that he would be coming back. Floyd, you see, believed in reincarnation.

Chapter 11
"Machine Gun" Kelly Misfires in Texas

The hysterical wife of an Oklahoma oilman called J. Edgar Hoover at home in the wee hours of July 23, 1933, to tell the head of the Bureau of Investigation (BOI) that her super-rich husband had been kidnapped. At that very moment, the victim lay bound and blindfolded in the back seat of a sedan speeding toward the Red River. Even with no pursuers in sight, George "Machine Gun" Kelly kept the pedal to the metal. He could not wait to show his wife, Kathryn, that for once he had done something right.

"Machine Gun" was born George Francis Barnes in 1895 into a comfortably middle-class family in Memphis, Tennessee. He even attended college for a couple semesters before eloping with a coed from his hometown. But the marriage hit the rocks after George turned a part-time passion for peddling bathtub booze into a full-time job as a bootlegger.

It took only a few trips downtown in a police car for George, probably at the urging of his mortified relatives, to change his name to Kelly and wander out west. He did a brisk business in Santa Fe until a bootlegging bust landed him in the New Mexico state prison in 1927. Freed less than a year later, he looked around for a location with a more tolerant climate and settled on a wide-open boomtown in Oklahoma.

George may have been, as he bragged many years later, "the king of the rumrunners" in Tulsa "with a good clientele [and] a good living," but he had not learned the importance of keeping his head down. Convicted again on bootlegging charges, this time in federal court, he was sentenced to two years in Leavenworth.

This mug shot of George Kelly shows that Kathryn did not have much to work with.

In a penitentiary full of well-known criminals, George was the smallest of small fries. But there was something about the petty bootlegger that Harvey Bailey liked, and the so-called King of the Heist Men took him under his wing. When they were released at the same time, Bailey took George along with the promise of teaching him a better-paying trade.

The wide-eyed novice helped the old pro rob a fat bank in Minnesota of $70,000 in July 1930. When one member of the gang got greedy and killed two others for their shares, George headed back south with every intention of returning to his former and far safer occupation. But he missed the turn at Tulsa and kept on going to Fort Worth. It was in Cow Town that he walked into a honky-tonk and met "the prettiest redhead I ever saw" who would change his life forever.

Thrice-married Kathryn Brooks Thorne was living it up on her dead husband's money. Bootlegger Charlie Thorne was found dead with a bullet in a vital organ and a neatly typed suicide note. Authorities brushed aside the troubling fact that Thorne was totally illiterate and could not write a word and ruled that he had taken his own life.

Kathryn had come to Texas in 1920 with her baby girl Pauline and her mother, Ora Shannon. Ora had tossed over Kathryn's biological father for

Robert "Boss" Shannon, a Wise County rancher who raised cattle only as a cover for his real business: selling sanctuary to outlaws on the run for fifty dollars a night. Kathryn attracted men like moths to a flame in the nightclubs and illegal watering holes of Fort Worth. One of her gentleman callers recalled nostalgically that she "took me to more speakeasies, bootleg dives and holes-in-the-wall than I thought there were in all of Texas. She knows more bums than the police department. She can drink liquor like water, and she's got some of the toughest friends I ever laid eyes on."

After a short and white-hot courtship, twenty-six-year-old Kathryn made thirty-five-year-old George Kelly husband number four in September 1930. At his ambitious bride's insistence, George graduated from bootlegging to bank robbery. He withdrew $40,000 from a bank in Sherman in April 1931 and the following February stole an undisclosed sum from another bank in Denton.

But there was not enough glamour or money in bank jobs to satisfy Kathryn. The really big bucks and banner headlines were in ransom kidnappings, fast becoming the latest thing in the underworld. In January 1932, she pushed poor George into grabbing the grown son of an Indiana banker. The asking price was $50,000, but his father would not come across. The victim finally bought his freedom with a worthless promissory note, much to the embarrassment of the kidnappers.

Kathryn decided George needed a gimmick and a clever nickname. She bought him a used Thompson machine gun at a Fort Worth pawn shop and made him take target practice every day at "Boss" Shannon's ranch. The next step was to start calling him "Machine Gun" Kelly, which quickly caught on.

When a beer baron's family paid the Barker-Karpis Gang $100,000 for his safe return in June 1933, Kathryn announced it was time to give kidnapping another try. With George and their partner, Albert Bates, she picked the target and planned the abduction down to the last detail.

Charles Urschel was a rags-to-riches success story of the first order. Teaming up with Texan Tom Slick, the Ohio farm boy made a colossal killing in the Oklahoma oil fields. After Slick dropped dead from a heart attack, leaving his children $15 million, Urschel married his ex-partner's widow and moved to Oklahoma City.

The Urschels were playing cards with another couple on that warm summer night when George and Bates suddenly materialized on their screened porch. When the foursome refused to point out the intended victim, the kidnappers took both men with them. The multimillionaire evidently identified himself and convinced George to discard the excess baggage.

The plan was sound, but the execution left a lot to be desired. George ran out of gas and had to wait on the side of the road for an hour while Bates walked to the nearest station. Later that night, whoever was driving fell asleep and ran into a ditch. But they eventually arrived at the ranch with their precious prize.

Four days after her husband's disappearance, Mrs. Urschel heard from the kidnappers. A family friend would board the express to Kansas City with a satchel containing $200,000 in small bills. At the instant a second signal fire was sighted, the courier was instructed to toss the bag off the train.

Mrs. Urschel did her part, but George failed to light the fires on schedule, and the bag man carried the cash to the end of the line. The ransom was later paid in broad daylight on a Kansas City street but only after George promised that the hostage would be home within twelve hours. With the golden egg in hand, Kathryn ordered George to kill the goose. For the first time in their one-sided relationship, the hen-pecked husband defied his domineering wife. He had given his word that Urschel would be released unharmed, and he intended to keep that promise, come hell or high water.

George might have thought twice about letting the oil tycoon live had he known about his phenomenal memory. Charles Urschel could remember everything—names, faces, places, all the trivial details of everyday life. During his debriefing by federal agents, he recalled hearing an airplane pass overhead at the same time twice a day. Checking the regular flights over North Texas, investigators correctly deduced Urschel had been held somewhere in Wise County.

Information supplied by Fort Worth police led the BOI straight to the Shannon Ranch. Charles Urschel, packing his personal shotgun, went along on the lightning raid of August 12, 1933, that caught the kidnapping crew napping. Everybody, that is, but the Kellys, who had departed days earlier without leaving a forwarding address.

Kathryn and George put hundreds of miles on a string of cars in their frantic attempt to stay one step ahead of their pursuers. The itinerary of their eight-week flight read like a travel brochure: Cleveland, St. Paul, Omaha, San Antonio and myriad points in between. In the mistaken belief that his hometown would be the safest place to hide, George talked Kathryn into going to Memphis.

Kathryn came unglued when she read in the newspapers that her beloved mother had been scooped up in the raid on the ranch. Without her husband's knowledge, she paid a homeless farmer to carry a secret message to the federal prosecutor. Kathryn offered to hand over George in exchange for a short sentence for herself and immunity for Ora. The feds had a good laugh and did not bother to reply.

Increasingly distraught over the plight of her poor old mother, Kathryn browbeat George into mailing a signed letter to the same prosecutor. "Machine Gun" threatened "the extermination of the entire Urschel family" unless he yielded to Kathryn's demand. But, alas, that did not do the trick either.

In the end, the Kellys hung around Memphis too long. Federal agents from Birmingham surrounded the house where they were staying on the night of September 26, 1933. They broke down the door to find "Machine Gun" Kelly sitting alone in the living room. He held out his hands for the cuffs, while Kathryn screamed her head off in the bedroom.

According to FBI folklore, the first words out of George's mouth were, "Don't shoot, G-men!" That was J. Edgar Hoover's official story, and he stuck to it. But a Memphis cop who was not beholden to a bureaucrat in Washington claimed Kelly was not nearly so melodramatic. All he reportedly said was, "I've been waiting for you all night."

George and Kathryn were hustled onto an airplane for a nonstop flight to Oklahoma City, where the government was wrapping up its case against Ora, "Boss" Shannon and his boy "Potatoes," Allen Bates, Harvey Bailey and seventeen other defendants. It ended three days later in convictions for every last one of them and prison terms ranging from life for the major players down to a minimum of ten years for the supporting cast.

At the time of their capture, the Kellys had little of the ransom payment with them. Even after $70,000 was recovered from a Coleman County, Texas ranch, roughly half of the $200,000 was never accounted for.

Kathryn and George were tried together in the same Oklahoma City courtroom as their friends, relatives and associates. "Dressed to the nines," to use Depression slang, Kathryn posed on and off the stand for the horde of photographers who could not get enough of her. Meanwhile, dumpy "Machine Gun" sat slump-shouldered at the defense table, scarcely showing any interest in the proceedings and obviously resigned to his fate.

Jurors enjoyed Kathryn's performance but refused to believe such a strong-willed woman was her husband's terrified pawn. Both were found guilty and given matching sentences of life in prison. As George was dragged away in chains, Kathryn called out sweetly, "Be a good boy."

By Alcatraz standards, George was a very good boy indeed, so well behaved that his hard-core neighbors changed his famous nickname to "Pop Gun Kelly." Before his transfer to Leavenworth, where he died from a heart

Kathryn and "Machine Gun" Kelly at their 1933 kidnapping trial.

attack in 1954 on his fifty-ninth birthday, the broken-down badman wrote a final letter to Charles Urschel: "These five words are written on the wall of my cell. Nothing can be worth this!"

Feet-first was also the only way Kathryn could expect to leave her lockup. But rather than admit in open court that it was George who had written threatening letters to the Urschels and not Kathryn, as the prosecutor argued at trial, the FBI consented in 1958 to her immediate release, along with her mother.

Kathryn and Ora tried hard to stay out of sight, but a persistent reporter found them four years later living and working under new names. "Why can't they just leave us alone?" Kathryn protested. Pressed for an explanation of her actions in the 1930s, Kathryn was ready with a self-serving rationalization of her criminal past: "I was just a young farm girl when I met Kelly back in 1930. I wasn't used to all the money, cars and jewelry George offered me. Any girl would have been swept off her feet same as I was."

And who knows? Over the years, Kathryn Kelly may have convinced herself that fairy tale was the truth and nothing but the truth. She even may have gone to her grave in 1985 believing her own pack of lies.

Chapter 12
Bandit Brothers in the Big Thicket

In the southeast corner of the Lone Star State is a remote realm known as the Big Thicket. Few Texans have ever seen it, and fewer still live in this out-of-the-way region, even in the twenty-first century.

The Big Thicket is a miniature Appalachia with dense and, in places, impenetrable vegetation instead of mountains. Even nowadays, only natives can find their way through the tangled interior without getting hopelessly lost. Many of those hardy inhabitants trace their roots back to the 1830s, when the first white settlers set up housekeeping on the fringes of the "Bear Hunter's Thicket," a description inspired by the astounding abundance of deer, panthers, wolves and, of course, bears.

No two people have ever been able to agree on where the Big Thicket starts and ends. The modern dimensions are roughly forty miles long and twenty miles wide, with the center in Hardin County northwest of Beaumont. That is what's left of the Big Thicket after the lumber industry and oil companies got through with it in the first half of the 1900s.

Thomas Jefferson and Darius Goleman did not see much of their father growing up in and around the Big Thicket. He was a traveling horse trader who rode around East Texas leading a string of his latest acquisitions. Since the elder Goleman was in the business of buying and selling, he did not ask his customers how they came about their horseflesh.

Eager to prove himself, like most young men in their teens, Thomas Jefferson, called "Red" because of the color of his hair, left home in the late '20s. Jobs for the uneducated and unskilled were easy to come by in the oilfields, making it possible for him to support himself and send a few dollars to his mother every now and then. Hard as the labor was for the roughneck, it did not provide the ego boost he needed. Red found that in bare-knuckle brawls, according to Dolph Fillingrin's rambling reminiscence printed verbatim in the book *Big Thicket Legacy*: "Red wanted the reputation of being the best fighter in every boom town he went to. Just like a doctor or a lawyer hanging out his sign, Red hung out his sign that he could whip any man in town."

At five-foot-ten and 175 pounds, Red did not always come out on top. But it went against his grain to accept defeat, and he would keep fighting the same opponent night after night until he whipped him.

While working on a Gulf Coast rig near Corpus Christi, Red picked a fight with a bigger and older man. The match ended tragically, with the other fellow dying from the beating the young bruiser gave him. Deciding to do the right thing, Red went to the sheriff and told him what had happened. A manslaughter charge was filed and bond set at $3,000, neither of which came as a surprise. What he had not anticipated, however, was the need to hire a lawyer to represent him at trial, and a good attorney cost money the roughneck did not have.

Since there was no bank in the state of Texas that would grant him a loan, Red picked the second-best option. He would rob a bank, and he knew which one: the fat little bank in Hull just over the Liberty County line.

When it came to reconnaissance, the rank amateur proved to be a fast learner, though a mite unorthodox. As Dolph Fillingrin told it, "He put on women's clothes and went to the Hull State Bank and stood around learning the routine. One man, after it all was over, said, 'I wondered about that woman. I saw her standing out in front of the bank, and she raised one foot like a man will and propped it back against the wall. A woman won't do that, but a man will.'"

Red noticed the bank was nearly deserted every day during the lunch hour. So on July 26, 1939, between noon and one o'clock, he walked in the door with a stand-up friend named Francis Smith. They hustled two female tellers, the only employees on duty, into the vault and took their sweet time emptying the cash drawers of $12,000.

The rookie robbers were long gone when a customer strolled into the building. Believing the workers were in the back, he joked in a loud voice, "Where is everybody? This would be an ideal time for a bank robbery!"

Red buried most of the loot in a jug in the Big Thicket and the rest in small amounts at several of his favorite locations. Then he found a place to hide and waited to see if the law came looking for him.

"Red" Goleman, "Texas Public Enemy Number One." *RGD5f4542 Houston Public Library HMRC.*

Two weeks in the Big Thicket, living on berries and other nutritious treats on Mother Nature's menu, gave Red a lot of time to think. Robbing the bank had been a stupid mistake, but maybe the sheriff would forgive and forget if he returned the stolen money. But the county cop was not in a forgiving, much less forgetful, mood. He locked Red up and let him out only for closely supervised hikes through the Big Thicket to the underground riches. To test the lawman, Red started out small, turning over $200 or $300 at a time. When this charade failed to win his freedom, he faked a bad case of amnesia and waited for a reduction of his bond.

As soon as the price of his ticket out of jail came down to a reasonable amount, Red had a reliable relative retrieve one of his larger stashes. But he skipped his January 29, 1940 court date and suddenly found himself "Texas Public Enemy Number One."

As if he did not have enough trouble already, Red let his younger brother talk him into a fool's errand. Darius wanted to pay a visit to a Beaumont cabbie who had been abusing his sister. The Golemans phoned in a request for a ride and jumped the driver when he came to pick them up. They drove the taxi into the countryside, beat the man to a bloody pulp and shot him once before heading for home. The cabbie survived, but the kidnapping and attempted murder charges turned up the heat on Red.

In a 1974 newspaper interview, Amos Laird, one of Red's legion of relatives, recalled him showing up at his house late that night in the stolen yellow cab. He heard a car door slam, and "about the time I could turn around T.J. was coming in the door. He gently took the baby from my wife's arms and held her close to his chest patting her on the back of the head.

"'I don't have to worry about the law shooting me through a window as long as I hold the baby close,' T.J. said to me." The man and his wife never felt quite the same toward their outlaw kinsman after that.

Alarmed as they were by Red's behavior, the Lairds did not have the heart to close their door to him. He came back one evening to eat supper with them and listen to the radio. The program was interrupted by a news bulletin warning the audience to be on the lookout for Red Goleman, who in the past hour had beaten, robbed and kidnapped a motorist in Galveston County.

Red stared down at the floor for a minute or two before looking up at his host. "Amos, they are going to blame me for everything that happens from here on. I'm a goner. I just don't have a chance," he said, sounding for the first time like a beaten man.

Then his eyes flashed with the familiar old fire. "One thing's for sure, though. They will never take me alive. I am never going back to jail."

Red disappeared into the trackless Thicket that he knew like the back of his hand. When he was not staying with sympathetic friends and blood relations, the now-famous fugitive was sleeping in a camouflaged shelter and living off the land.

An army of man-hunters swept the Thicket over and over again without finding a trace of their elusive quarry. Although the pursuers never knew it,

Red was almost in their grasp at least three different times. Trackers once came within a few yards of the runaway before he fled across a vast swamp. On another occasion, they passed so close to his homemade shelter that he could have reached out and touched them. Still another time, unsuspecting officers questioned Red's grandmother as he hid in her attic.

A tip in April 1940 led the laws back to the grandmother's farm near Kountze. According to the official report, they staked out the place for days and observed a steady stream of people go to and from a corncrib out back. Convinced they finally had their man, they made their move. While a deputy held everybody in the house at gunpoint, the sheriffs of Hardin and Jefferson Counties and two other deputies cautiously approached the wooden shed. Red Goleman was given one last chance to come out with his hands up but chose instead to start shooting. The four lawmen opened fire, filling the corncrib with hot lead. Detecting neither sound nor movement in the shed, they reached in and pulled out the dead body of the most wanted man in Texas.

Red's aunt related a fundamentally different version of his final moments in a conversation with the Baytown newspaper thirty-four years later. Addie Ewing's story went like this:

> T.J. was standing in the yard talking to all of us when he seemed to see something and hollered at us, "Watch them laws!" He ran to the corn crib, slammed the door behind him and everybody started shooting everywhere. T.J. didn't even have a gun.
>
> One of the lawmen jumped up on the porch and stuck a gun in my stomach so hard that it knocked me backwards. When the shooting stopped, that lawman made us all go into the house and I could hear Agnes screaming from the porch, "They've killed my son."
>
> Then they gathered up every gun in the house and took a mattress and blanket off one of my beds and took it out to the crib. They propped the guns up against the crib and put the mattress inside. By the time a photographer from Beaumont got here, they had the crib looking like T.J. had been sleeping in there but he hadn't.

A Beaumont undertaker came and took the body away. When he opened for business the next day, hundreds of people were already standing in line, waiting their turn to see Red Goleman in the dead flesh. The viewing went on without a break until three o'clock in the morning and resumed at daybreak. The funeral director was later quoted as saying that in thirty-six hours as many as ten thousand individuals from as far away as Missouri and Mississippi filed past the open casket.

When the minister at Red's funeral dared to say, "As ye sow, so shall ye reap," those in attendance could not resist glancing in the direction of the guest of honor. Red might have taken that remark as an insult, and it would have been just like him to climb out of the coffin and kick that preacher's butt.

After the service, several hundred people walked or drove the two miles to the farm for an up-close and personal peek at the bullet-riddled corncrib. Red's aunt Addie charged them ten cents a head for the privilege at a time when a dime could actually buy something. Addie could have put a deposit down on a headstone for Red with the money she made off the "tourists," but she didn't. That was how Red Goleman wound up in an unmarked grave that over the years went missing.

The Jefferson County sheriff refused to grant Darius Goleman, who was being held on charges related to the cab driver attack, "compassionate leave" to attend his brother's funeral. It was a common practice in Texas in those days, and the sheriff's decision struck many people as cruel and unnecessary, especially after the case was dismissed due to a lack of evidence.

That was one cause cited by those who knew Darius best for his full-blown life of crime after Red's death. Baby brother was determined to follow in big brother's footsteps. But the senseless and unprovoked murder of a housewife he had never laid eyes on seemed completely out of character for Darius. He was arrested in June 1949 for beating to death a woman who had given him a ride. Red's well-known record and the murder convictions of two uncles helped to persuade the grand jury that Darius was just another rotten apple from the same barrel. Convicted on the basis of a signed confession, which too late he recanted, Darius was sentenced to die in the electric chair in December 1952.

To the bitter end, Darius stuck to his story that the cops beat a false confession out of him. But he would not give his executioners the satisfaction of seeing him turn into a sniveling coward at the appointed hour. As Darius Goleman plopped down in the chair, he growled at the guards, "Pull those damned straps tight and give me all the juice you got because I'm not going to die easy."

Brother Red would have been proud.

Chapter 13
Fun and Games in Galveston

It stands to reason that the narrow strip of sand off the coast of Texas that served as a pirate stronghold in the early 1800s would wind up a mecca for the seekers of forbidden pleasures in the middle of the twentieth century. The difference between Jean Lafitte and the bootleggers, flesh peddlers and gamblers who turned Galveston into America's first "sin city" was that they had much more to offer and far more staying power.

The way Islanders prefer to remember it, everyone had a good time and no one got hurt. The prostitutes on Post Office Street, for example, were part of a rich and tolerant tradition dating back to the Civil War. A census of sorts conducted in 1943 counted eleven brothels, eight hundred "working girls" and a syphilis rate three times the national average.

Then came Prohibition and a brand-new cash cow. The Texas legislature ratified the Eighteenth Amendment to the U.S. Constitution on the last day of February 1918 and a short time later made Texas a bone-dry state two full years before Prohibition became the law of the land. True to form, Galveston remained a public watering hole where anyone with the price of a drink could wet his whistle. The Twenties were just starting to roar when the island emerged as a major point of entry for illicit liquor. Regular as clockwork, smugglers in high-powered speedboats rendezvoused with foreign freighters full of contraband alcohol. Hundreds, sometimes thousands, of cases a week were secretly slipped ashore for overland shipment to speakeasies throughout Texas and as far north as Detroit.

Two criminal organizations fought for control of this high-profit pipeline: the so-called Beach Gang, led by Dutch Voight, and the Downtown Gang, headed by the menacing George Musey and colorful Johnny Jack Nounes. While Voight wisely maintained a low profile that enabled him to stay on the street, Nounes spent almost as much time in jail as the limelight he adored.

Johnny Jack's free-spending flamboyance earned him folk-hero status among admiring Galvestonians but also attracted the unwanted attention of federal agents, who succeeded in sending him to Leavenworth in 1924. Less than two years after his triumphant return, Nounes and his partner, Musey, were caught red-handed at Seabrook with a boatload of booze.

"It's in again, out again, caught again," moaned Johnny Jack after the judge slapped him with a long penitentiary sentence. In contrast to Nounes, who was resigned to his fate, Musey skipped bail and fled to Canada to avoid going to prison.

When the fugitive picked Fatty Owens to run the Downtown Gang in his absence, disgruntled lieutenants broke ranks and formed rival factions. A bootlegger war soon broke out, complete with hijackings and periodic bloodshed. In late February 1931, Owens tried to bring in three trucks of spirits from Beaumont. Despite the presence of armed guards, gun-toting thieves stopped the caravan fifteen miles east of Houston and made off with the entire shipment.

Two weeks later, Kye Gregory and Mitch Frankovitch, former members of the Nounes-Musey mob and prime suspects in the highway robbery, accepted Fatty Owens's invitation to a bury-the-hatchet powwow. The meeting was held in the back room of a soft-drink stand in downtown Galveston. At the end of the short and seemingly friendly get-together, the two guests shook hands with Owens and his associate Jimmie Crabb. But before they reached the exit, someone shouted, "Stick 'em up!"

Kye Gregory took a bullet in the shoulder and a second round in the abdomen. He staggered outside and collapsed on the sidewalk, to the horror of lunch-hour pedestrians. Meanwhile, Mitch Frankovitch squeezed between two parked cars and traded shots with Owens crouched in the alley.

About this time, two foot patrolmen arrived on the scene and shouted at the combatants to cease firing. Both meekly complied, as if they had been waiting all along for someone to tell them to stop. Owens surrendered on the spot, telling officers as he handed them his smoking gun, "They tried to get me, but they'll pay hell doing it." His sidekick Crabb made a clean getaway but turned himself in at police headquarters later that afternoon.

Bleeding profusely from a chest wound, Frankovitch begged Chief of Police Tony Messina to drive him to the hospital. The top cop rushed the bootlegger to the emergency room, where doctors determined the bullet had ricocheted off his breastbone, barely missing his heart. Frankovitch would live, but his partner in crime was not so lucky. Kye Gregory was dead on arrival.

At his trial for the murder of Gregory, Fatty Owens took the stand to insist he abhorred violence. "I don't even like to kill a bird," he swore pitifully. The defendant claimed the killing was a terrible accident. When the shooting started, he pointed his gun, closed his eyes and squeezed the trigger.

The jury returned a verdict of guilty, but the testimony of prominent character witnesses watered down the prison term to a token two years. The police chief and a city commissioner went to bat for Owens, describing the notorious gangster as a law-abiding pillar of the community, which in Galveston eight decades ago may not have been far from the truth.

The downtown shootout was but the latest violent incident in a bloody fight-to-the-finish in Galveston's gangland. James Clinch survived four attempts on his life, but on October 5, 1929, he was killed by a shotgun blast in the back. Two years later, the lifeless body of Sam Lachinsky was dumped on the beach from a moving car.

Sam Maceo did a convincing imitation of a respectable businessman. *RGD5f3427 Houston Public Library HMRC.*

108

The void created by the departure of Johnny Jack Nounes and George Musey and the body count from the bootlegger war was filled by two Sicilian brothers, Sam and Rose Maceo. Barbers by trade, they moved to Galveston from New Orleans on the eve of the First World War and soon discovered there was much more money to be made in booze, gambling and nightclubs than cutting hair. With the opening of the Hollywood Dinner Club in 1926, the Maceos were on their way.

Sam was the brains and Rose was the brawn. Sam was the genial, impeccably dressed host at the Hollywood, where he booked big-name entertainers like Phil Harris, who became a close personal friend and convinced other well-known performers to come to Galveston.

Camera-shy Rose rarely spoke but could strike fear with his chilling stare. During the Depression, his name came up in connection with a number of murders, including that of a "civilian" in 1933. A young pilot named Lee Hausinger, thought to have robbed a Maceo employee, died from a bullet in the chest the night of the alleged crime. Before he expired, Hausinger named Rose Maceo as his killer. As a rule, juries tend to attach a great deal of importance to deathbed identifications, but not in Galveston in the 1930s. Rose's automatic acquittal was par for the course.

In 1935, George Musey returned from exile fully expecting to pick right up where he had left off. But the Maceos did not tolerate competition, especially from a veteran criminal who knew what he was doing, and decided Musey had to go. A Maceo underling by the name of Windy Goss took care of the dirty business, shooting the intruder five times. The case went to trial, but the jury accepted Goss's claim that he was acting in self-defense.

The slaying that caused the Maceos the most trouble and jeopardized the very future of their undisputed reign took place on Christmas Eve 1938. Had the Yuletide victim been just another shady character, the murder would not have tarnished anybody's tinsel. Over the years, the epidemic of underworld homicides had conditioned easygoing Galvestonians to casual carnage, which they shrugged off so long as the back-alley boys killed their own kind.

But twenty-four-year-old Harry T. Phillips was no underworld figure. The popular assistant engineer at the Galveston Ice and Storage Company chose December 24 to announce his engagement to a student nurse. After dining with friends at a seawall restaurant, he saw his fiancée home and returned for a nightcap.

Perched on a stool next to two dinner companions, Phillips was suddenly accosted by a belligerent baritone. "This is my chair, buddy. Do you mind?"

Galveston chief of detectives Willie Burns (left) and police chief William Whitburn (right). *RGD5f6605 Houston Public Library HMRC.*

Two Maceos with the same name: Vic. *RGD5f6605 Houston Public Library HMRC.*

snarled Leo Lera, a minor minion in the Maceo organization. Eyewitnesses would differ on the exact wording of his reply, but Phillips muttered something in response. Whatever he said set Lera off like a Roman candle. The muscular thug punched Phillips in the face, knocking him to the floor. Staggering to his feet, the last thing the groggy groom-to-be ever saw was the chrome-plate .45 automatic in the hoodlum's right hand. Four ear-splitting gunshots left the restaurant in panic-stricken pandemonium and young Phillips in a sea of his own blood. Lera stood transfixed, seeming to admire his handiwork, before calmly walking out the door. Gingerly loaded into a private car, the unconscious Phillips was rushed to the hospital. Meanwhile, long after the smoke had cleared, the police finally put in an appearance at the scene of the crime.

On the ride to headquarters in a patrol car to give their statements, the two grieving friends spotted Leo Lera outside the Little Turf, the Maceo hangout where he tended bar. Along with Mike Calandra, also present at the shooting, Lera was huddled with Vic Maceo, a high-ranking family member. Calling Vic over to the car, the officers explained the sticky situation. Since their vehicle was filled to capacity, would the civic-minded Maceo mind driving the suspects downtown?

Lera and Calandra were halfway through the booking process when the telephone rang. Harry Phillips had died, changing the charge to first-degree murder.

Though a fifth-grade dropout, Leo Lera was not unschooled in the intricacies of life on the street. He had, after all, had sense enough to sign up with Sam and Rose Maceo instead of their second-rate competition. With the Maceo brothers in his corner, Lera figured he was an odds-on favorite to beat the rap.

One thousand tense spectators packed the courtroom on December 29, 1938, for the preliminary hearing. They listened in amazement as the defense counsel clumsily acknowledged his clients' guilt. The flustered attorney tried to cover his tracks by arguing the crime was a clear-cut case of manslaughter, punishable by no more than five years imprisonment, rather than murder, which carried a possible death penalty.

Four days into the new year, the grand jury decided that Lera alone should answer for the death of Harry Phillips. The trial was set for January 23, 1939.

On the witness stand, Leo Lera owned up to pulling the trigger but painted a dramatically different picture of events leading up to the gunfire. Dressed in the suit stained with his victim's blood, he swore his sidekick Calandra had fought with the deceased. Hoping to break up the brawl, Lera testified that he fired three rounds into the ceiling. Disavowing any desire to harm a perfect stranger, he swore Phillips lunged wildly for the pistol, causing the accidental discharge that killed him.

The jury did not buy the implausible story and in no time convicted Lera of murder. Three hours later, the same dozen came back with a death decree.

The conviction was overturned on appeal, as was the identical outcome of the retrial. But the third guilty verdict stuck, and not even a pair of last-minute reprieves could postpone the inevitable. In February 1943, Leo Lera was strapped into "Old Sparky" and given the shock of his life.

Long before the execution, it was business as usual in Galveston. The Maceos renovated the old Sui Jen, which reopened in 1942 as the Balinese Room, the swankiest casino west of Havana. For the Maceos, the cold-blooded murder of Harry Phillips was nothing more than a petty

The Balinese Room was the crown jewel of the Maceo empire. *RGD5f6605 Houston Public Library HMRC.*

annoyance. Once Leo Lera was on his way to Death Row, the clamor for a cleanup was drowned out by the din of the busy slot machines and the crowded craps tables.

Nineteen-year-old Herbert Cartwright rose to prominence as one of the leaders of the short-lived crusade that petered out after the Maceos shrewdly threw the expendable Lera to the wolves. When he stepped back in the public arena nine years later, it was not as an outspoken idealist dedicated to purging the island of the pimps and gamblers but as a cynical supporter of the corrupt status quo.

Cartwright unseated the incumbent mayor with a campaign pledge to establish "a regulated open town." "I don't believe in prostitution or kids gambling and drinking," he declared, "but when a man or woman gets to be 21 years of age, I don't worry about them."

One thing the boy mayor did believe was that Galveston was a world unto itself, a place where mainland laws did not apply. "We don't butt into the affairs of our sister cities," Cartwright told a Dallas audience, "and we don't want them to butt into ours."

But change was in the salt air after World War II. The free-spirited days of booze, brothels and blackjack on the outlaw island were numbered.

The Maceo machine lost Sam, its guiding genius, to cancer in the spring of 1951, three weeks before the state legislature opened hearings on the

Galveston mayor Herbert Cartwright (left) chats with future governor Price Daniel at 1951 hearings. *RGD5f6605 Houston Public Library HMRC.*

Opposite: Sam Maceo at a 1942 narcotics trial in New York. Federal prosecutors failed to convict him. *RGD5f7483 Houston Public Library HMRC.*

nefarious goings-on in Galveston. Lacking the dearly departed's gift for public relations, the gamblers and their cronies made a bad impression in Austin. Citing their Fifth Amendment right against self-incrimination, fourteen members of the Maceo organization refused to answer any questions from the special committee. Three even declined to give their names.

Herbert Cartwright and other local officials were more talkative. Following the mayor's impassioned plea for continuing the hands-off policy of the past,

the recently retired police commissioner summed up a lifetime on the island with a candor that stunned lawmakers: "Galveston was wide-open before I was born. It was wide-open when I came into office and I left it wide-open."

The most entertaining witness was Frank Biaggne, who was asked to explain why in nearly two decades as county sheriff he never busted the Balinese Room. "I go to the man at the desk and I say, 'How about getting in?' And he says, 'Nothing doing,'" answered Biaggne with a deadpan

The Galveston sheriff said he tried to raid the Balinese Room but could not get in this door. *RGD5f6605 Houston Public Library HMRC.*

Texas Ranger captain Clint Peoples's undercover probe shut down gambling in Galveston. *RGD5f6605 Houston Public Library HMRC.*

expression. "You see, my name is not in the book. I'm not a member. And then I just walk away."

Colonel Homer Garrison, director of the Department of Public Safety and head of the Texas Rangers, testified that a raid on the Balinese Room in 1947 taught him the futility of trying to enforce the law in Galveston. He said that in spite of "a perfect case" put together by the Rangers, the district attorney refused to accept the complaint because he did not want "to set a precedent."

"The people of Galveston seem to think because they live on an island they are immune from the laws of this state," concluded Garrison with visible anger.

The gambling joints temporarily closed for the hearings promptly reopened. But things definitely were not the same in Galveston and never would be again.

Attorney general and future governor Price Daniel obtained an injunction to cut the Maceo horse-racing wire and crippled their bookmaking racket. The legislature made possession of a slot machine a felony, resulting in the reluctant storage of one thousand one-armed bandits, and the IRS took many family members and associates to court for income tax evasion.

Mayor Cartwright lost his bid for reelection in 1955 to a challenger who promised worried voters that "gambling and prostitution will keep Galveston an 'isle of enchantment.'" But he was powerless to prevent the plug from being permanently pulled two years later on the island paradise of illicit pleasures.

Time has a funny way of playing tricks on people's memory, especially if they want to forget any past unpleasantness. In the half century since Texas attorney general Will Wilson and the Rangers shut down Galveston tighter than a drum, most Islanders have put the ugly side of the wide-open era behind them while romanticizing the night life that kept the tourists coming.

But in the end, the facts speak for themselves. All we have to do is listen.

Recommended Reading

Barrow, Blanche Caldwell. Edited by John Neal Phillips. *My Life with Bonnie & Clyde*. Norman: University of Oklahoma Press, 2005.
John Neal Phillips did the best job he could putting Blanche's version of her brief but bloody life with the Barrows in book form. The book's flaws are not Phillips's but Blanche's. She had a lot of axes to grind.

Guinn, Jeff. *Go Down Together: The True, Untold Story of Bonnie & Clyde*. New York: Simon & Schuster Paperbacks, 2009.
No one has amassed more research on the subject of Bonnie and Clyde than Guinn. But he is a journalist by trade, not a storyteller, and it shows. Also, Guinn's deep-rooted antipathy for those characters on the wrong side of the law muddies the water.

Hinton, Ted, as told to Larry Grove. *Ambush: The Real Story of Bonnie and Clyde*. Austin, TX: Shoal Creek, 1979.
This is the first Bonnie and Clyde book everyone should read. Grove does a masterful job of turning Hinton's disjointed recollections into a classic on the subject.

McComb, David G. *Galveston: A History*. Austin: University of Texas Press, 1986.
McComb is a rarity: a college professor who knows how to write for the nonacademic reader. I have waited almost three decades for a better Galveston chronicle to come along, and it has not happened yet.

Phillips, John Neal. *Running with Bonnie and Clyde: The Ten Fast Years of Ralph Fults.* Norman: University of Oklahoma Press, 1996.
My personal favorite for two simple reasons: Fults is a richly complex and compelling character and Phillips is an excellent writer. It is a winning combination for any reader.

Index

About the Author

Bartee Haile began writing "This Week in Texas History" in 1983 for small-town and suburban newspapers across the Lone Star State. Thirty years and nearly 1,600 columns later, it is the most widely read and longest-running feature of its kind *ever*.

Bartee also was a regular contributor to true-crime magazines back in the 1990s before the disappearance of that genre. He brings a deep understanding of Texas history and a keen insight into the criminal subculture to *Texas 7Depression-Era Desperadoes*.

A fourth- or fifth-generation Texan (he can't really say for sure), Bartee Haile lives in the Houston area with his wife, Gerri.